COSMIC TRIGGER
THE PLAY
BY DAISY ERIS CAMPBELL

Based on Robert Anton Wilson's

**Cosmic Trigger:
Final Secret of the Illuminati**

Introduction by
Ben Graham

Cosmic Trigger the Play by Daisy Eris Campbell

Copyright © 2021 Daisy Eris Campbell

All rights reserved. No part of this book, in part or in whole, may be reproduced, transmitted, or utilized, in any form or by any means, electronic or mechanical, including photocopying, recording, or by any information storage and retrieval system, without permission in writing from the publisher, except for brief quotations in critical articles, books and reviews.

International Standard Book Number (eBook): 978-1-952746-17-8
International Standard Book Number (Print): 978-1-952746-09-3

First Edition 2021, Hilaritas Press
eBook Version 1.0, 2021, Hilaritas Press

Cover Design by Polly Wilkinson
Book Design by Pelorian Digital

Photographs by Jonathan Greet,
with additional photographs by Simon Annand,
Elspeth Moore and Dan Sumption

All rights whatsoever in this play are strictly reserved and application for performance by professionals and amateurs should be made prior to commencement of rehearsals. Rights may or may not be available at the time of application. No performances may be given unless a license has been obtained. Applications should be made to Hilaritas Press:
info@hilaritaspress.com

The author graciously thanks the following
for permission to adapt prior work into this stageplay:
The Robert Anton Wilson Trust (*Cosmic Trigger trilogy, Illuminatus!*)
The Robert Shea Estate (*Illuminatus!*)
The Ken Campbell Estate (*Illuminatus!* theatrical adaptation)
Chris Langham (*Illuminatus!* theatrical adaptation)
Adam Gorightly (*The Prankster and the Conspiracy*)

Hilaritas Press, LLC.
P.O. Box 1153
Grand Junction, Colorado 81502
www.hilaritaspress.com

For my Cosmic Sisters

Michelle Watson
Kate Alderton
Claudia Boulton
Michelle Olley
Nadia Luijten

TABLE OF CONTENTS

Introduction by Ben Graham XI
Review from *London City Nights* XXVII

ACT ONE

1.1 THE GATES OF ETERNITY 3
1.2 THE TWO BOBS MEET 13
1.3 ERIS INTERRUPTS 20
1.4 DISCORDIAN INITIATION 26
1.5 BURROUGHS AND WATTS' VISIT 39
1.6 HOME FROM THE CONVENTION 54
1.7 MULDOON AND GOODMAN 58
1.8 VISIT TO MILLBROOK 62
1.9 BOB'S FIRST ACID TRIP 68

ACT TWO

2.1 GATES OF ETERNITY 87
2.2 1994 91
2.3 PLAYBOY OFFICES 99
2.4 NEW ORLEANS – 1957 116
2.5 ARRIVING AT THE NEW HOUSE 123
2.6 BOB'S BIRTHDAY MORNING 127

2.7 THE MORNING AFTER 156
2.8 MOON INTERLUDE 158
2.9 SIRIUS CONTACT 160
2.10 LUNA PAINTS THE WHITE LIGHT 166
2.11 LIVERPOOL PERFORMANCE 1976 177
2.12 FINISHING *ILLUMINATUS!* 184

ACT THREE

3.1 ANOTHER ERIS INTERRUPTION 188
3.2 A VISIT TO LEARY IN PRISON 195
3.3 CROWLEYMAS 208
3.4 THE MORGUE 222
3.5 THE PARTY'S OVER 223
3.6 FUNERAL 231
3.7 LIVERPOOL PERFORMANCE 233
3.8 GRIEF AND POVERTY 237
3.9 THE NATIONAL THEATRE 241
3.10 ON STAGE 246
3.11 BLACK MASS SCENE 249
3.12 FINAL WORD 256
CAST & CREW 266

Introduction

By Ben Graham

When I was about 10 years old, at a village primary school in West Yorkshire, I invented a game that got out of control. I can remember almost nothing about what that game involved, except that it was more like a play, in the most basic sense of the word. I came up with the outline of a story, or a scenario, perhaps with characters that were on different sides, and me and my small group of friends started playing it.

Now, I wasn't a particularly popular child. I was bright enough to feel different, but wasn't conventionally smart or committed enough to ever be top of my class. I was shy, lived in my imagination and was completely disinterested in sports, when almost all of the other boys I knew were football crazy. And by this time I was approaching the age when you start only really hanging out with your own gender, even though I'd been close friends mostly with girls a few months before. So the little gang of pals I had at this point in my life was made up of the handful of other odd boys who didn't like sport; the misfits that nobody wanted on their team.

I mention this only to make clear that I wasn't a leader or a trend-setter at school, and our ragged bunch wasn't one that other children ever wanted to emulate or be a part of. I came up with the game because we were left out of everything else. I can't remember if there was an objective, or even if the game had any rules to speak of. All I remember is that it quickly caught on.

Other children, boys and girls, became intrigued by what we were doing. For the first time in our lives, we were interesting. We were almost envied. We had a secret, and the regular kids who'd always looked down on us wanted in. They wanted to be part of our play, and of course we let them. Over an incredibly short time, maybe a week, it got bigger and bigger. It splintered into different groups: all playing the same game but slightly differently, independent of each other while still loosely interacting. The game, the play, grew more complex. It sprawled out over the whole field. And then one day I came out of dinner late, and went down to join in the game, only to find that I no longer recognized it, and it no longer recognized me.

Nobody remembered where the game had started, and nobody knew where the game would end. I still joined in, but it wasn't mine anymore. It was everybody's, and to be honest, I was a bit miffed. But I was also amazed, because this was when I first realized that this was what stories, games, and especially plays could and would do, if they were strong enough. They would take over as many imaginations as possible, because that was how they came alive. The author is only the original host: a launching platform from which the story-play-game-virus moves on to bigger and broader things.

Daisy Campbell's theatrical adaptation of Robert Anton Wilson's *Cosmic Trigger* is another play that got out of control. In this case the weird kids, with their niche, esoteric, chaotic creation, attracted other weird kids – but there were far more of them than anyone knew or suspected. Like other epoch-defining counter-cultural events – the International Poetry Incarnation at the Royal Albert Hall in 1965, or the Sex Pistols at Manchester's Lesser Free Trade Hall in 1976 – the first performance of *Cosmic Trigger,* at Camp & Furnace in Liverpool on November 23, 2014, was where a particular group of people found and recognized themselves, in the audience and on stage, and realized that they weren't alone.

I use the term 'kids' loosely, by the way. This isn't generational: those caught up in *Cosmic Trigger's* slipstream range from teenagers to seventy-somethings, and most of us have been around the block a few times. We've been part of other scenes, picked up a few tricks and survival skills, but for whatever reason we'd never truly found our people – until now.

Just as the Albert Hall poetry reading kicked off the UK psychedelic underground, and the Pistols spread the germs of punk wherever they played, so everyone that saw *Cosmic Trigger* took a piece of the play away with them. In more cases than is usual, people were inspired to create work of their own, and in the case of a crucial few, the play changed their lives. But most importantly, for almost everyone that saw it, *Cosmic Trigger* helped them Find The Others. And with each new happening, work of art, piece of fiction, poem, song, concept or pilgrimage that followed, more Others were drawn into the Mycelium – the invisible, underground web of connections of which the

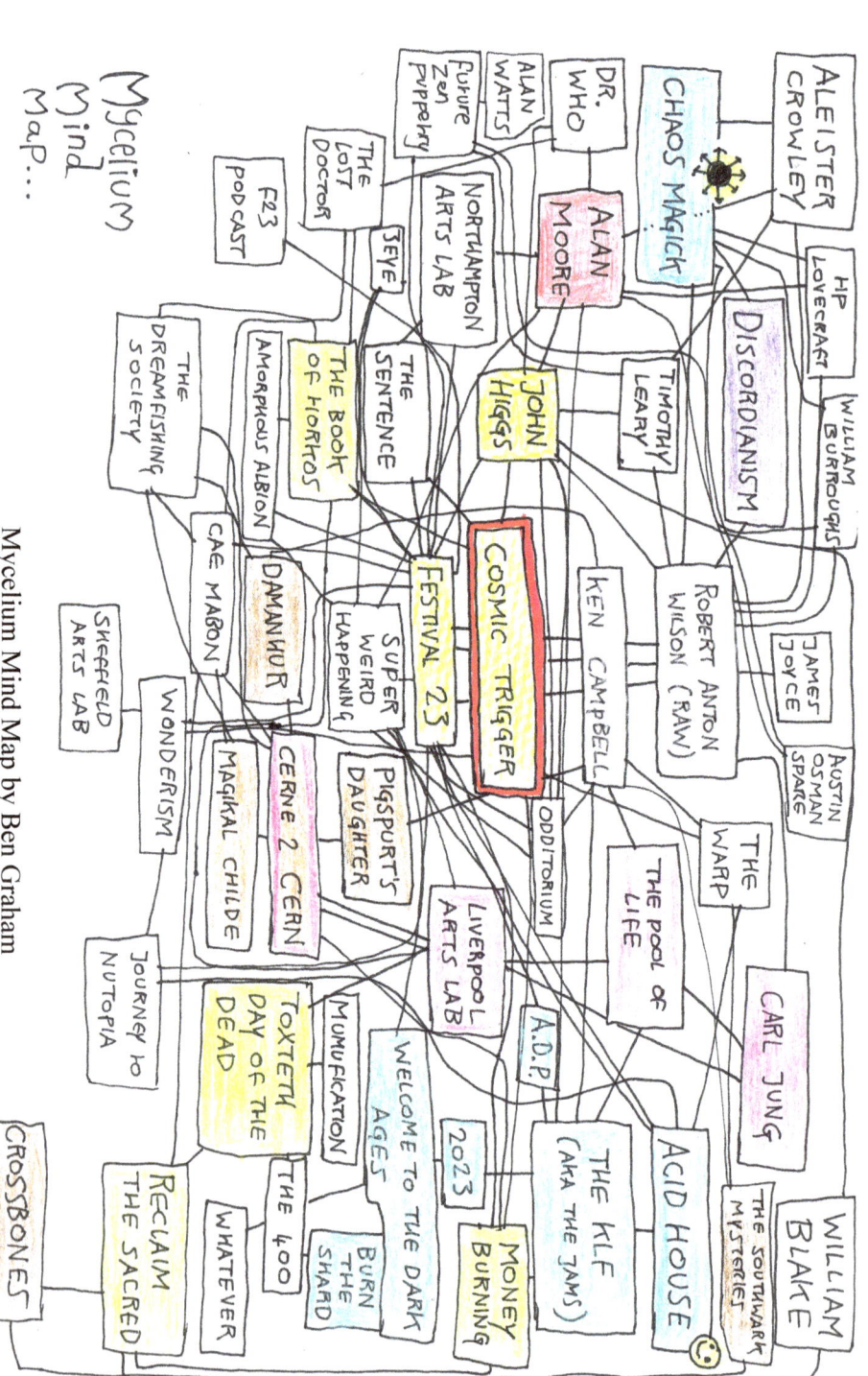

Mycelium Mind Map by Ben Graham

metaphorical mushrooms that sprout up are only the visible manifestations, made possible by the far more widespread, surging creative network beneath.

But why *Cosmic Trigger*? Why should this play, based on a 37-year-old book by a cult American author, a book dealing with events and people remote in time, space and cultural context, prove such an explosive catalyst in twenty-first century Britain? Well, for one thing, Daisy's *Cosmic Trigger* is far from a straight adaptation, which would have been impossible anyway. It's a brilliant original work, that takes elements of the book, elements of RAW's life, and ideas from a multitude of sources, and synthesizes them into a fresh creation which, in "bringing back realities that are supposed to be dead" manages to be both relevant and revolutionary. But also, the initial seeds had been planted a generation earlier.

In the mid-1970s, Liverpool poet Peter O'Halligan dreamt of a spring bubbling forth from the manhole cover at the end of Mathew Street, where several roads met. On visiting the location he found an old warehouse that was available for rent, and turned it into an affordable café and second-hand market, where like-minded souls could meet, talk and dream. Among other things, this was where the Liverpool punk scene hatched. Later, O'Halligan found that the warehouse was built over an ancient spring.

Soon after, O'Halligan read Jung's *Memories Dreams Reflections,* in which the eminent psychoanalyst revealed that in 1927 he too dreamed of Liverpool, which he'd never visited, and a small, sunlit island surrounded by a pool of water in a spot where several roads met. Jung identified Liverpool as the Pool of Life, and O'Halligan identified Jung's dream with his own, and believed that it too was set at the end of Mathew Street. He placed a bust of Jung on the outside wall of his market/café, and named the building the Liverpool School of Language, Music, Dream and Pun. O'Halligan then decided to open a small theatre in the building, and for its first production commissioned a new play from the eccentric experimental theatre director Ken Campbell.

The play that Campbell debuted in Liverpool in November 1976 was a nine-hour adaptation of RAW's *Illuminatus!* During the initial run, Ken became involved with the actor Prunella Gee, who played the goddess Eris among other roles. In March 1977, *Illuminatus* transferred briefly to the National Theatre in London, and in September 1978 Ken and Prunella's daughter, Daisy Eris Campbell, was born.

Ken Campbell went on to many further capers, and his whirling energy drew all kinds of kindred spirits, fools and brilliant mavericks into his orbit, but he never returned to *Illuminatus,* RAW or Discordianism. There had been too many casualties and too much dangerous weirdness around the play even for this dedicated seeker after the strange and bizarre. However, in 1987, Bill Drummond (the former Liverpool art student who'd been set designer on *Illuminatus!*) and Jimmy Cauty (a musician and artist who'd seen the play in London) formed a situationist hip-hop duo called The Justified Ancients of Mu Mu, AKA the JAMs, who a couple of years later evolved into the chart-topping pop-rave act The KLF. Steeped in imagery and ideas drawn both directly and unconsciously from *Illuminatus,* The KLF enjoyed a run of massive hit singles, critical acclaim and high media visibility before spectacularly terminating their career with a notorious performance at the 1992 Brit Awards and, in 1994, ridding themselves of the proceeds of said career by burning a million quid in a boathouse on the Isle of Jura.

The *Illuminatus* references went unnoticed by most that bought the KLF's records, and were rarely mentioned in the music press. But some got them, and some (like me) were inspired to seek out and read the original book as a result. Meanwhile in post-punk and then the underground rave scene the number 23 popped up with suspicious frequency, and acts like Spiral Tribe and Psychic TV certainly knew their RAW onions. Add in a continuous occult underground, revitalized by the highly RAW-influenced trend known as Chaos Magic that manifested in West Yorkshire in the late seventies, and was swiftly disseminated through various media including the mass market science fiction kids' comic *2000 AD,* and it's clear that a neo-Discordian current was bubbling under in the UK from 1976 through to the end of the century at least, sometimes lurking in the shadows and sometimes (as with The KLF) hiding in plain sight.

Rave and acid house culture influenced the late-nineties revival of *The Warp,* staged first at the Albany Theatre in Deptford and then at a number of venues, most notably the catacombs beneath London Bridge station. Ken Campbell had originally directed this impossible 23-hour play cycle, written by poet Neil Oram, in 1979. 20 years on, it became his 19-year-old daughter Daisy's directorial baptism of fire, and also first brought together many of the actors, enablers, visionaries and genii-without-portfolio who would be integral to *Cosmic Trigger* and the community that grew out of it, including producer Michelle Watson, Oliver Senton (who took the lead role in both plays), Kate Alderton (Arlen), and Claudia Boulton, who made the part of Eris her own.

RAW died in 2007, and Ken Campbell died in 2008. Afterwards, Daisy was repeatedly approached to restage *Illuminatus* but always declined, feeling that she wanted to do something new, or at least a play that would be a bridge between her father's work and her own. She later claimed that deciding to adapt *Cosmic Trigger* wasn't entirely her idea; that to some extent the universe had maneuvered her into doing it.

In 2012, John Higgs published his breakthrough book, *The KLF: Chaos, Magic And The Band Who Burned A Million Pounds*, which made explicit the links between the half-forgotten band, Robert Anton Wilson and so much more. Inevitably, Campbell and Higgs connected (it didn't hurt that both lived in Brighton, the south coast city that's something of a sanctuary for bohemian non-conformists and creative thinkers). Higgs introduced Campbell to the writer and wizard Alan Moore, best known for ground-breaking comics like *Watchmen, V For Vendetta* and *From Hell*. A long-term RAW aficionado, Moore explained his concept of magic to Daisy: that art and magic are essentially the same thing.

As Daisy later recalled it, "there's high art and high magic, and high magic is when you don't know what the hell you're doing, but you just proceed as though everything around you is a sign or a message." From this point on, *Cosmic Trigger* was conceived as an explicitly magical act; a Fool's Leap, and a shout into the void that would hopefully receive a reply.

The first person Daisy approached was Michelle Watson, as an invaluable co-pilot and experienced producer, whose Warp initiation meant that she would be prepared for the Herculean task ahead. A core team soon formed, tackling everything from crowdfunding to hunting down discordians who could make props and costumes. As well as Daisy and Michelle, this group included Dominic Search, Michelle Olley, Scott Mcpherson, Claudia Boulton and Nadia Luijten.

Meanwhile, Campbell and Higgs hit the campaign trail. The project was announced at a Night for Robert Anton Wilson at London's Horse Hospital on October 23, 2013. Having been rejected for Arts Council funding, Daisy turned to the amorphous Discordian community for help in putting the play on, while not knowing for sure if such a community existed. It did: the crowdfunder was officially launched on May 23, 2014, and raised over £23,000 in six weeks. There were further talks and scratch performances of scenes from the play-in-progress in London, Nottingham and Brighton, and one in Liverpool that included a magical ritual at the manhole cover in Mathew Street, where Cat Vincent invoked Alan Moore's fictional working-class magician John Constantine, and a pair of rainbow knickers were ceremonially placed on the bust of Carl Jung's head.

Cosmic Trigger was finally performed in full on the weekend of November 23, 2014, as part of a three-day 'Conferestival' at Liverpool's Camp & Furnace venue, that also included talks, films, sideshows, live bands and DJs, and a full Discordian Papal Ball after the riotous four-hour play. Speakers included Robert Temple, Adam Gorightly, Dr David Luke and Robin Ince; performers and DJs included Nina Conti, Youth, Greg Wilson, John Constable and more. *Cosmic Trigger* then transferred to the Lost Theatre in London for a four-night run to November 29. Forget your coat, luv: the Cosmic Trigger's pulled.

Those of us that saw *Cosmic Trigger* in 2014 left the

theatre knowing that we'd been charged with a mission. Not just the prime directive to Choose Love Over Fear (though that proved an essential – if largely ignored – guide to navigating UK politics, and the Brexit referendum, over the next few years), but also to Find The Others. As Daisy explicitly states in the script, appearing as herself: "Why are we doing this show? Because in the words of Timothy Leary, once you've turned on, tuned in and dropped out, the next thing you gotta do is find the others. What others are we finding? The ones who have also realized that it's all a play."

The Conferestival had already proved a more wonderful and extensive gathering of others than the many who thought they were the only remaining Discordians on Planet World could ever have hoped for. It couldn't, however, be just a one-off. This was the impetus behind Festival 23: Convergence of Disco, a three-day outdoor music, arts and magic festival, with camping, which took place near Sheffield on the weekend of July 23, 2016. Taking its cue from *Cosmic Trigger's* combination of profound philosophical wisdom and joyously pantomimed silliness, Festival 23 aimed for a similar blend of the sublime and ridiculous, and it all got marvelously messy indeed.

I was one of eight directors on F23's 'Veering Group', but we were guided and supported by a wider co-operative of equals, 'Notwork 23', essentially formed from many of the others that *Cosmic Trigger* drew out of the weirdwork, and other others besides. Festival 23 was fully collaborative in the widest possible sense, and also fully immersive, with no distinction between performers and audience, organizers and attendees, reality and imagination. There were no innocent bystanders: we were all making it up as we went along.

Daisy and her gang were at Festival 23 in full effect, presenting a multi-faceted Cosmic Trigger Cabaret that occupied much of the main stage on the Sunday. There was also a read-through of a new play written by Daisy, the first pledge in the Cosmic Book of True Will, later to be renamed the Book of Horkos. This book came into being at the Gathering of the Cosmic Fools, held exactly one year after *Cosmic Trigger,* as a way for participants to escape "the lovely quicksand of the imagination" and manifest their creative projects in the universe. Once a pledge is written in the book, it must be achieved by the next signing (typically six months) otherwise the whole volume is burned. I pledged to complete my Discordian novel, *Amorphous Albion,* under the eye of Horkos, and at the time of writing, The Book survives and continues to enforce its implacable discipline.

From The Fool to The Universe: as Simon Moon says in the play, "We've gotta get into Tarot, man… the whole key to liberation is magic," though of course the deck needs to be read in reverse order. There are 78 Keepers of the Cards, individual guardians of Daisy's own Thoth deck, ready to be called in to serve at any moment. There is also the Pilgrim's Tarot, representing the 69 pilgrims who traveled with Daisy from Cerne Abbas in Dorset to CERN in Switzerland in April 2019, via the underground temples of Damanhur and Carl Jung's Bollingen Tower, to immanentize the eschaton and birth a magical childe… but that's another story, and is mentioned here only to demonstrate how long, deep and strange this trip has become.

Indeed, by the time a slightly-revised *Cosmic Trigger* was restaged by Daisy at London's Cockpit Theatre for

23 nights in May 2017, not only had many of us realized that it was all a play, we also realized that the play had never ended, and that we'd been living inside the reality of *Cosmic Trigger* for much of the past two-and-a-half years. Some of us, myself included, had also definitely gone through the experience RAW calls Chapel Perilous. Be warned, this is very real; and although in my experience *most* people seem to come out okay, it's a bumpy journey and can take some time.

As Bob Shea says in the play, "We've unleashed some weird shit, no doubt about it." From the Money Burner's Manual and the Church of the Cosmic Burn to a four-hour continuous read-through of Alistair Fruish's incredible unpunctuated novel *The Sentence*; from further F23 events around the country to Super Weird Happening and Reclaim The Sacred; from the resurgent Arts Lab movement to the Dreamfishing Society and Richard Norris's Journey to Nutopia, the web of connections around *Cosmic Trigger* keeps on growing.

Over the week of August 23, 2017, The Justified Ancients of Mu Mu (formerly The KLF) returned with *Welcome To The Dark Ages,* a five-day happening on the streets of Liverpool, directed by Daisy and featuring *Cosmic Trigger's* Oliver Senton as The Officiator. The event provided the barest framework within which the 400 ticket-buyers (who swiftly identified themselves as simply The 400) became not merely observers but active co-creators of the experience, and went on to generate new musical, literary and artistic works of their own.

As a result of *Welcome To The Dark Ages'* perfectly staged pay-off, each November 23 is now not only the Discordian Holy Day and birthday of Harpo Marx, or the anniversary of *Illuminatus* and *Cosmic Trigger,* but the annual Toxteth Day of the Dead, on which the People's Pyramid slowly rises. Anyone that signs up for 'mumufication' will have 23g of their ashes baked into a brick after they die, and will become a part of that pyramid.

Mumufication is a joint venture between the JAMs and the Green Funeral Company, AKA Ru and Claire Callender, who as Ways With Weirds presented talks and performances as part of the wider programming around both the 2014 and 2017 *Cosmic Trigger* performances. At the Ways With Weirds event during the 2017 run, John Higgs coined the phrase "pessimism is for lightweights" which Salena Godden turned into a poem that captured the imagination of the nation. On the closing night, Cat Vincent (borrowing a term from Jeanne and Spider Robinson) suggested that we should self-define as "rapturists", the opposite of terrorists, a concept that Higgs (at a later F23 event) renamed wonderism, and which others then refined, developed and put into practice.

The point is that all of this is open-ended and collaborative, and also that there is an unbroken chain of transmission. From RAW to Ken to Daisy and onwards; back to Leary and Burroughs, Carl Jung and even Aleister Crowley; these individual contributors may live and die, go in and out of fashion, achieve great heights and fail just as spectacularly, but they remain part of an ongoing, multi-generational community of free thinkers, outcasts and seekers in a narrative so complex and self-referential that it becomes, to all intents and purposes, alive. So while *Cosmic Trigger* may recap ideas and stories from the 1960s and '70s, it is also our story, now, and it's here for you to be a part of too.

Reality is what you can get away with, and the initiation never ends. Maybe you've always been playing a game that got out of control. Maybe you started it, but forgot it was just a game, or joined in because everyone else was playing and it seemed like there was no alternative. But once you remember it's just a game, or a play, it's still possible to change the rules, pick a new part, or simply flip the board in the air and walk away. And then you find the others, and you write a better story together; and suddenly life becomes a whole lot more interesting.

Want to know more? Then inquire within…

Ben Graham
July 23, 2020

Review from London City Nights

By David James

Thus far, 2017 is a grey, chilly void. May is here but the darling buds are nowhere to be found: cemented over by unseasonally frozen winds, deprived of energy by a slate grey prison of an overcast sky, and trampled on by huddled masses who can't believe they're still having to put a fucking scarf on to go to the shops.

Not to mention that (based on all current polling predictions) it seems as if this miserable May is here for the foreseeable future, presiding over a spiteful country hellbent on flushing itself down the economic, political, and humanitarian plughole. We're staring down the barrel of a shitty future and the present ain't too hot either.

All this makes me deeply appreciative of *Cosmic Trigger*, the theatrical equivalent of someone pounding a syringe of adrenaline into my gloomy heart. It's a primary coloured explosion of optimism and intelligence, delivered with sincere joy and a sincere love of humanity.

Ostensibly an adaptation of Robert Anton Wilson's memoir

Cosmic Trigger: The Final Secret of the Illuminati, Daisy Eris Campbell's play winds and curls through Wilson's text like a worm munching through an apple, chronicling the intellectual and spiritual evolution of the counterculture author (Oliver Senton), whose seminal conspiracy adventure books *The Illuminatus! Trilogy* (co-authored with Robert Shea) have subtly woven themselves into the popular consciousness.

We first meet him as editor of the *Playboy* forum advice column, a position which brings him into contact with heavy hitters like William Burroughs, Timothy Leary, and Kerry Thornley (among others). The psychedelic culture propels him towards an esoteric magickal and political awakening via Crowleyian occultism, a process which alters his brain, causing him to reject the concept of objective truth.

But that's just the bleached skeleton of *Cosmic Trigger* - and it's the flesh surrounding it that's oh-so-juicy. This is a night that opens with a striptease from a goddess, features a man wildly fucking a giant inflatable apple, has a hovering shark swimming across the stage, cunnilingus on a female Stretch Armstrong, and... well. I could go on, but it'd be a sin to spoil the night's many delights. This one show has more interesting stuff going on than a whole *season* of other plays, each scene coming complete with its own idiosyncratic pleasures - be they dramatic, visual, or musical.

Whether we're in 1950s New Orleans, a mushroom party for magicians and technocrats, backstage at a Liverpool theatre, within a vast secret submarine or the cosmic depths of Wilson's mind, the show keeps a firm hand on the thematic tiller. As far as I can see this is primarily because

Cosmic Trigger's playwright has a supremely confident grasp on Robert Anton Wilson's philosophies. Then again, given that she was apparently conceived backstage *during* Ken Campbell's groundbreaking 70s theatrical adaptation of *Illuminatus!,* if anyone's going to successfully map out this tangled territory it's her.

The play is composed of many tangled threads which eventually braid together into an exaltation of Wilson's optimistic conclusions: that social, sexual, and psychological limitations are largely imposed from within, that humanity has the ability to shed restrictive dogmas and ideology, and that reality is exceptionally mutable. Having this lesson taught so vividly made me feel like a drowning man finally thrusting his head up from the depths to gulp a full lungful of air.

I originally came at Wilson via a meandering trajectory that began watching *The X-Files* as a kid, which led me to *The Fortean Times,* which in turn led me to many of my all time cultural icons: Alejandro Jodorowsky, Chris Morris, Alan Moore (whose unmistakable voice and face appears throughout *Cosmic Trigger*), Grant Morrison (specifically *The Invisibles*) and to Wilson himself, whose writing blew my (at the time somewhat chemically addled) mind.

Cosmic Trigger combines this panoply of influences into a singular experience - a distillation of mental rebellion against a system that damn near everyone realises is completely fucked, yet ticks along because nobody can think of anything better. For brief moments, this play allows us to imagine that 'anything better', the Cockpit Theatre all-too-briefly becoming a glimmering bubble of illumination amidst the miles of beaten down concrete.

There are times when you sense that *Cosmic Trigger* is merely the latest ripple in a ritual that's been gradually unfolding for generations - a through-line that began at Crowley and wound through the 60s counterculture, passing authors like Burroughs, Wilson, Dick, and Moore, through Ken Campbell's Science Fiction Theatre of Liverpool, the music of the KLF, and finally, tonight, to the Cockpit Theatre. The play bears this cultural weight with grace and style.

Perhaps this isn't the most objective of reviews - I went in a fan of Robert Anton Wilson and, let's face it, any play that features Alan Moore as a supercomputer called FUCKUP is going to be hard for me to resist - but this was one of the most enjoyable, uplifting and entertaining plays I've seen in quite some time. The cast are all fantastic, the stagecraft is phenomenal, and the writing is sensitive, witty and (when it needs to be) outright heartbreaking. *Cosmic Trigger* is a real triumph of theatre: boisterously beating back the grey, dystopian miseries of Trump, Brexit and alllllll the rest.

xxx

Cosmic Trigger
The Play

ACT ONE

1.1: THE GATES OF ETERNITY

Candles, scent, smoke. An ornate arch with heavy red curtains and THE GATES OF ETERNITY above in ominous lettering.

Haunting music. A beautiful Goddess walks slowly and deliberately through the audience towards the Gates of Eternity. She is dressed in a simple robe and sandals. On top of her head sits a thousand petaled crown.

A strange glow emanates from behind the curtains.

NB: In our productions, Ishtar was played by a different volunteer every single night.

FUCKUP
(Just a booming voice)

It was a sad time after the death of the fair young god of spring, Tammuz. The beautiful goddess, Ishtar, who loved Tammuz dearly, followed him to the halls of Eternity, defying the demons who guard the Gates of Time. At the first Gate, the guardian demon forced Ishtar to surrender her sandals, thereby giving up her Will.

> Ishtar removes her sandals and continues to walk towards the Gates of Eternity.

And at the second Gate, Ishtar surrenders her jewelled anklets, which the wise say means giving up Ego.

> She does so

Now she must surrender her robe. This is the hardest of all because she is giving up Mind itself.

> Slowly Ishtar lets her robe drop to the floor. Beneath it she wears a bejewelled golden breast plate. Her long hair just covers her naked buttocks.

At the fourth Gate she surrenders her golden breast cups, thus giving up Sex Role.

> She removes the breastplate.

Next she surrenders her necklace, and forever gives up the rapture of Illumination.

> She does so

At the Sixth Gate she surrenders her ear-rings, giving up Magick.

> She does so. She is now nearing The Gates of Eternity.

And finally, at the Seventh Gate, Ishtar surrenders her thousand-petaled crown, by which she gives up Godhood.

> She removes her crown and stands naked before the curtains. The music becomes increasingly discordant, and a great wind blows the curtains up, and Ishtar's hair with it, revealing her nakedness.
>
> The lettering above the Gates rearranges itself into the words CHAPEL PERILOUS. Behind the blowing curtains lurk all manner of creatures and characters - amongst them: a green man, a silver space woman, a pookah, Aleister Crowley in full ceremonial dress and a dog-faced Sirian alien.
>
> A blinding light emanating from the curtains renders the creatures shadowy and hard to see.

Ishtar surrenders, arms wide.

The music is now almost unbearable – jarring and too loud. As it reaches a hellish crescendo, the creatures' hands grab at Ishtar's naked body. For a desperate moment Ishtar struggles to escape, but she is gripped too tightly. A hellish sucking noise almost drowns out her screams as she is pulled to her destiny.

Then all is quiet and still.

>FUCKUP
>(loud and portentous)

It was the year when they finally immanentised the Eschaton . . .

Rising organ music . . .

>WILSON
>(entering)

Hold on! Hold on!

Through the curtains, gesturing for quiet, steps Robert Anton Wilson. He's a sexy intellectual sci-fi type in his late 30s with a goatee and a twinkle in his eye.

The Voiceover scratches to an abrupt halt.

WILSON

We can get to all that immanentising of eschatons in a little while. Right now I think it's about time I introduced myself. My name is Robert Anton Wilson. And it is from my head that all this confusion (Hail Eris!) doth emanate. I mean, I am really Oliver Senton.

(actor speaks in own voice)

And I actually speak like this,

(back to Wilson's Brooklyn drawl)

but we're prepared to overlook that fact tonight and enter my reality tunnel, right?

After all, as somebody said: "art is lies that look like truth." Certainly, since Surrealism and Orson Welles, art and life, and art and magick, have never gotten clearly disentangled again to the satisfaction of all observers. So – this lie-dressed-up-as-truth that we embark upon tonight is:

FUCKUP (V.O.)

Cosmic Trigger: Final Secret of the Illuminati.

WILSON

As the late, great H.P Lovecraft might begin this narrative: It is now nearly 13 years since the ill-fated day when I first began investigating the terrible legends surrounding the enigmatic Bavarian Illuminati, an alleged conspiracy that some people believe rules the world. What I was to discover is that in researching occult conspiracies, one eventually faces a crossroads of mythic proportions, called Chapel Perilous in the trade. And you emerge either paranoid or agnostic.

WILSON

Aleister Crowley, everyone.

> MUSIC: A song from Aleister Crowley, an accordion playing spectre, who is accompanied by the strange creatures from Chapel Perilous.

CROWLEY
(sung)

I slept with Faith and found a corpse in my arms on awakening
I drank and danced all night with Doubt and found her a virgin in the morning

ALL CREATURES

On virgin or pigeon
We place no reliance
Our goal is religion
Our method is science

> The creatures repeat their refrain with increasing intensity, leering menacingly at the audience. As Crowley hits the final note they disappear like smoke.

WILSON

If you go into that realm without the sword of reason you will lose your mind, but at the same time, if you take only the sword of reason without the cup of sympathy you will lose your heart. Even more remarkably, if you approach without the wand of intuition, you can stand at the door for decades never realising you have arrived. You might think you are just waiting for a bus, or wandering from room to room looking for your cigarettes, or watching a cryptic and ambiguous play.

> As Wilson talks the creatures form a gelatinous human chain behind him. After a beat the awful creature hands grab him all over, and he too is pulled into Chapel Perilous. A beat.

LUNA
(appearing elsewhere)

In this play it is spoken of the Sephiroth and the paths, of spirits and conjurations of Gods, spheres, planes and many other things which may or may not exist. It is immaterial whether they exist or not. By doing certain things certain results follow; students are most earnestly warned against attributing objective reality or philosophical validity to any of them.

1.2: THE TWO BOBS MEET

The *Playboy* offices, Chicago – 1968

Wilson is sorting piles of letters at his desk. Around the office are many mailbags, all spilling over with yet more unsorted letters.

Robert Shea enters and approaches him.

SHEA

Hi, you're Bob right? So am I. Bob . . . as well. Nice to meet you. So apparently I'll be working with you on the forum stuff.

WILSON

Oh yeah? I hope you're prepared for some seriously crack-pot correspondence.

SHEA

I have an open mind.

WILSON

After doing this job for a while you might want to close it up again.

SHEA

So what exactly should I do?

WILSON

Well a little while back we published a request for "exposés" – stuff that had been suppressed in the mainstream press. We promised that startling submissions would be well paid.

(gesturing to the mailbags)

Here's the results of that request. Who killed JFK is in that corner, Alien abductions over there, this one is Vatican bankers, Marilyn's here (God rest her sweet soul), fluoride mind control is this bunch here. So – get sorting.

SHEA

Ok . . . What are you working on?

WILSON

I take the mail and write the Playboy official response to it. Straight-up do-your-own-thing liberalism. But where I can I like to sneak in a some anarcho-pacifist propaganda.

Shea nods, taken with this idea

Just do it in the voice of the readers, though, right? At the moment I'm working on this *Who Owns Erik Whitethorn* series. You know this story? Mrs Whitethorn, has sued the government for trying to draft her son, Erik who's 18. She claims she owns Erik until he reaches 21, and that the government could therefore not take him from her.

SHEA

So does this kid belong to himself, to his mother or to the pentagon?

                    WILSON
                    (impressed)

Exactly! It's just a magic trick on the collective unconscious, most people think that five-sided castle literally owns them and their offspring, just like they think they *owe* money to the IRS.

                    SHEA

So I have to ask, does Hugh Hefner really sleep with all the bunnies? Or is he homosexual?

                    WILSON

Sorry to disappoint you, Bob. Hugh is definitely not homosexual, and I wouldn't say he sleeps with all the bunnies.

>   Shea starts to flick through the letters.

                    SHEA

What's this one?

"I recently heard an old man of right-wing views – a friend of my grandparents – assert that the current wave of assassinations in America is the work of a secret society called the Illuminati. He said that the Illuminati have existed throughout history, own the international banking cartels, have all been 32nd degree Masons and were known to Ian Fleming, who portrayed them as Spectre in his James Bond books – for which the Illuminati did away with Mr Fleming."

>   Wilson smiles enigmatically and pulls out a previously hidden, enormously stuffed mailbag.

                          WILSON

Yeah, we've had quite a few about the Illuminati recently.

                           SHEA

There's nothing in it though?

                          WILSON

Fourth most common organised paranoia, after

    (Pointing to mailbags of increasingly smaller sizes)

Elders of Zion, Jesuits and Government control by aliens.

                           SHEA

And I thought this job would be all extramarital affairs and dating etiquette.

                          WILSON

Ha. There's some college kids in Berkeley who've reformed the Bavarian Illuminati – been quite busy firing off letters and press releases. Sophomore humour.

                           SHEA

So . . . I guess we won't bother answering that one, then?

                          WILSON

I don't know. Give me that.

                        MUSIC: A little "ding" – indicating this is an important idea.

I might do a little digging around – see if I can throw up anything about this Illuminati enigma. Beyond what these nut jobs keep sending in.

SHEA

Wow! This one is really nuts. I love it. The headed paper says: "The Bavarian Illuminati – the world's most successful conspiracy". From Mad Malik.

WILSON

AKA Kerry Thornley.

SHEA

Kerry Thornley?

WILSON

AKA Omar Ravenhurst. AKA The Goose of Limbo.

SHEA

Nut job?

WILSON

Of the best kind. He publishes a little magazine called The New Libertarian. He's been sending me a whole batch of Illuminati related letters. Sometimes they're from the Illuminati themselves, sometimes they're from this other group, the Discordians.

SHEA

Discordians?

WILSON

Yeah, from what I can gather it's a group Kerry's formed that worships Eris, Greek Goddess of Chaos and Confusion.

SHEA

Oh wow – listen to this:

(Reading)

"a pox upon the accursed Illuminati of Bavaria, may their seed take no root. May their hands tremble, their eyes dim and their spines curl up, yea, verily, like unto the backs of snails; and may the vaginal orifices of their women be clogged up with Brillo pads"

WILSON

Yeah, that's one of his – I hope.

Momentary pause.

SHEA

So are there more of these Discord –

WILSON

Discordians. I think it's basically Kerry and his pal Greg Hill. I'm meeting the two of them next week. You want to come? They had a vision in a bowling alley in which Eris revealed herself to them.

SHEA

She's not an actual Greek Goddess though, is she?

WILSON

I'm not sure. I think so. Wasn't there something to do with her throwing an apple or something?

1.3: ERIS INTERRUPTS

> Suddenly, ripping through the reality fabric of the play itself, there stands the Goddess of Chaos and Confusion herself.

ERIS

Stop this show! This is complete bullshit. You invoke my name without even knowing whether I'm for real? You foolish, foolish mortals. Before the night is through you'll wish you'd chosen your gods with more care.

ACTOR OF WILSON
(in his own voice and accent)

No, no. It's fine.

> She turns her glare on him, and he cowers.

We know who you are really, great Eris Goddess of Discord. We were just acting. Can we please resume our humble play?

ERIS

No, you can't. I'm going to do my play. You clearly all need educating. Make space!

Eris points to a man in the audience. A plant.

NB in London we had the plant enter as hapless latecomer, whose phone then rang. As he fumbled desperately to switch it off, he slowly realized that Eris was looming over him.

Well you can be my idiot father Zeus. Ok. And who can play my stupid sisters?

She picks out three women from the audience. Real audience members.

OK, Zeus – you say that I'm not invited to your shitty little party up on Mount Olympus. Then I get a bit angry, and throw the Golden Apple of Discord and you three fight over it. You're Athena, Hera and Aphrodite – no better make you Aphrodite – Oh this is a farce. Anyway, my apple says "to the prettiest one"

(indicating the woman she's pulled from the audience)

Hahaha that's a joke! So you all fight because you all want to be the prettiest one, OK?

OK. Action.

                (to the plant playing Zeus)

Say: "I can't come to your party."

ZEUS
(pathetically)

I can't come to your party.

ERIS

Oh for goodness sake, get it the right way around: "I can't come to your party."

ZEUS

You can't come to my party?

ERIS

Oh by the horns of Horkos, say it like you mean it!

ZEUS
(with true zest and feeling)

You may not enter through the door to Mount Olympus, for you are not welcome at this party.

ERIS
(fully in character, enraged)

WHAT DID YOU SAY?!

(breaking character)

Give me my Golden Apple of Discord!

> No apple appears.

ERIS

Whichever mortal is responsible for delivering my apple to me had better start trembling.

> Actors and crew run about in search of the apple.

ERIS

Right, while this bunch of incompetents find my apple, let's run over the rules of this game. When they throw in the apple – you three goddesses are going to fight over it, OK? I mean fight like fuck.

> At that moment an enormous inflatable Golden Apple with Kallisti written on it is thrown in (ideally from high above), which bounces into the audience.

ERIS

Fight, fight, fight! You all want to be the prettiest one, don't you? You wish you were don't you madam? Well, get your claws in there then woman, you get that apple and I promise you will be! Fight fight fight!

> Total chaos ensues. The cast encourage shouting out the

> Goddess's names, jeering, booing, hissing etc. Pure panto.

ZEUS
(now clearly an actor)

OK, we'll settle this once and for all.

(aside)

I'm not getting dragged into this debate. We'll ask a mortal.

(He indicates a real audience member)

You sir. Choose your Goddess. Who is the prettiest?

(stage whisper)

Choose Athena, she'll keep you undefeated in battle.

ACTOR OF WILSON

Choose Hera, she'll give you all the riches in the world.

ERIS

Choose Aphrodite. She'll give you the most beautiful woman in the world.

> Encouraged by Eris and the others, the audience shout and chant for their favoured Goddess. Aphrodite wins.

ERIS

OK, since the most beautiful woman in the world is Helen of Troy and she's shacked up with the King of Sparta we're going to have to unleash war on Sparta. What will later become known as The Trojan War. Said to be the first war amongst humans. Oh well. That's what you get for not inviting Chaos to the party.

Go on then, get back to your little play. I'm the educational part of the show. You won't forget my story again in a hurry.

1.4: DISCORDIAN INITIATION

Wilson's home – 1968.

A pleasant home, warmly furnished with evidence of small children. Many well-stocked bookshelves.

Kerry Thornley and Greg Hill, two wild looking gents, are pacing in Wilson's living room, inspecting his books.

KERRY

You see this, Greg? This guy's got more books on the Illuminati than's healthy.

GREG

Maybe he's the head of the Illuminati.

KERRY

Yeah, tricked us into coming over to find out what we know.

Arlen, Wilson's red-headed wife appears in the door holding a baby. She watches the two men a little suspiciously for a beat.

ARLEN

Can I get you gentlemen anything?

KERRY AND GREG
(sweet and polite)

No thank you ma'am.

> Arlen exits. Wilson enters with joint-rolling wherewithal.

WILSON

So I'm assuming some Mary Jane will be an important factor in this initiation?

KERRY

For sure.

ARLEN
(Popping in on her way out)

I'm taking Graham for his check-up. Luna's upstairs. You'll keep an ear out?

WILSON

Sure, my love. This is Greg Hill and Kerry Thornley.

ARLEN

Nice to meet you both. I'm Arlen.

WILSON

They're going to initiate me in to the Church of Discordia.

KERRY

That's right, ma'am. The world's first true religion.

ARLEN

Sounds fun. Keep an ear out, OK?

>			She exits.

GREG

You know what your Discordian Pope name is going to be?

WILSON

Mord the Malignant?

GREG

Yeah, that'll do.

KERRY

So, by becoming a Discordian Pope you agree that God is a Crazy Woman and that Holy Chaos is the Natural Condition of Reality.

GREG
(receiving the joint)

If organised religion is the opium of the masses, then disorganised religion is the marijuana of the lunatic fringe.

WILSON

A non-prophet irreligious disorganisation.

KERRY
(to Greg)

I told you this guy was good. OK let's formally do this thing.

> Greg and Kerry dress Wilson up in various ridiculous elements from the room and their bag.

GREG

OK, first rule of Discordianism – we Discordians must stick apart. The most chaos can be created if not one Discordian knows for sure what another Discordian is up to.

KERRY

Yeah, but look out for Fang the Unwashed. He's excommunicated every Pope that we've managed to ordain.

GREG

You must partake of a hot dog every Friday, but hotdog buns are completely banned.

KERRY

What was your name again? Mordecai the Foul?

WILSON

That'll do.

KERRY
(in a booming, portentous voice)

Are ye a human being and not a cabbage or something?

> Bob Shea enters and stands watching, unnoticed by the others.

WILSON

Yes.

GREG AND KERRY

That's too bad.

GREG

Do you wish to better yourself?

WILSON
Yes.

GREG AND KERRY
How stupid.

KERRY
Are ye willing to become philosophically illuminated?

WILSON
Yes.

GREG AND KERRY
Very funny.

GREG
Will ye dedicate yourself to the Erisian movement?

WILSON
Probably.

GREG AND KERRY
Aha!

KERRY
Then repeat after me: Before the Goddess Eris, I Mordecai the Foul do hereby declare myself a brother of the Legion of Dynamic Discord.

WILSON
Before the Goddess Eris, I Mordecai the Foul do hereby declare myself a brother of the Legion of Dynamic Discord.

KERRY AND GREG
Hail Eris! All Hail Discordia!

WILSON

Hail Eris!

> They all fall back on the floor, satisfied. They re-light the joint.

Wow. So what happens next?

KERRY

The ceremony generally degenerates. Did you enjoy it?

WILSON

Yeah, it would be even better if I got to fuck an enormous golden apple.

SHEA

Hello?

WILSON

Bob! Come and meet Omar Ravenhurst and Malaclypse the Younger. Or Kerry and Greg. They've just initiated me in to the legion of Dynamic Discord.

SHEA

So I saw.

> Shea is passed the joint.

No, I don't – well, I never have. Well . . . Hail Eris I suppose . . .

ALL

Hail Eris!

> He takes a drag and has to sit down.

SHEA

So Discordianism is a complex joke disguised as a religion?

KERRY

No it's a religion disguised a complex joke. Shall we initiate you?

SHEA

Maybe later.

KERRY

Your loss! So, to business! Bob reckons he can publish some stuff in the Playboy forum about the Bavarian Illuminati.

> Kerry hands Wilson a few pages of writing.

SHEA

We're going to publish that letter? You're not serious?

WILSON

Seriousness is not a vice I possess. We're calling it Operation Mindfuck.

KERRY

It should be so convincing – all the Illuminati claims – that for years to come so-called intelligent people will be saying "But what if it really isn't a put-on?"

WILSON

I've been doing a bit of research. So the Illuminati was a movement of republican free thought founded on May Day 1776 by a guy called Adam Weishaupt, a former Jesuit. He made contact with various Masonic lodges, and an Illuminati convert often seems to have gained a commanding position. So it became like a secret society within a secret society. Then there was internal dissention and it was banned by an edict of the Bavarian Government in 1785.

SHEA

So the idea is to make it seem like it never actually went away . . . ?

WILSON

Exactly. And the great thing is, there's already a good deal of paranoia about the Illuminati out there – we just need to give it a little push.

SHEA
(unconvinced)

So this Operation Mindfuck thing is about spreading paranoia?

KERRY

Yeah, let's accuse everybody of being in the Illuminati. Nixon, Johnson, all the conspiracy buffs, everybody.

GREG

Ourselves.

SHEA

I don't know, Bob. You start telling these kids this kind of stuff and who knows where it'll lead. How will they know who to trust?

WILSON

The way I see it is if the New Left want to live in the reality tunnel of the hard-core paranoid, they have an absolute

right to that neurological choice. We'll just introduce so
many alternative paranoias that everybody can pick a
favourite.

GREG

That's it, Man!

WILSON

Let's call it Guerilla Ontology. Try and shake people out of
their fixed way of seeing the world so they might actually
think for themselves. Liberation through paranoia!

KERRY AND GREG

Liberation through paranoia!

SHEA

Liberation through paranoia? OK . . .

He gets up, and gets a
headrush.

Hey, what if the Discordians and the Illuminati were
actually locked in an ancient battle?

WILSON
(running with the idea, excitedly)

Going back to the Knights Templar.

KERRY

To the Greek and Gnostic Initiatory cults.

GREG

To Egypt.

WILSON

To Atlantis!

                           KERRY
                    (fucking a chair)
Get in some links with Nazis and Satanists.

                           SHEA
But hint that perhaps they're actually the good guys.

                           WILSON
Reality is what you can get away with!

                       KERRY AND GREG
Reality is what you can get away with!

                                    Kerry and Greg do the peace
                                    sign, holding up two fingers.

                           SHEA
               (indicating the sign that Kerry is doing)
What's that?

                           KERRY
It's the Discordian mystic sign. We lifted it from good old Tory Warmonger Winston Churchill.

                                    Wilson puts the joint into
                                    Kerry's upright fingers.

                           GREG
The fact that it's also used in blessings by Catholic Priests and by Satanists invoking the devil illustrates the ambiguity of all symbolism.

                           SHEA
Hail Eris!

                    WILSON, GREG AND KERRY
                         (doing the sign)

All Hail Discordia!

                              KERRY

Brothers of the Legion of Dynamic Discord – the time of
Operation Mindfuck is upon us. Let's fuck some minds!

                              MUSIC: Recording of Kick
                              Out The Jams by MC5 blares
                              loud as the cast hands out
                              Discordian propaganda.

NB: We handed out actual flyers for forthcoming Discordian events.

A video montage of Operation Mindfuck in action appears on the screens. Yippies campaigning for Pigasus, flowers in gun barrels, hippies flashing the peace sign and spinning footage of outrageous underground press headlines.

                WILSON
      (to audience, over the music)

Most Discordians at this time were contributors to underground newspapers all over the country. We planted numerous stories about the Discordian Society's aeon-old war against the sinister Illuminati. The Discordian revelations seemed to press a Magick button. New exposés of the Illuminati began to appear everywhere.

VT footage ends with Abbie Hoffman calling for everyone to come to Chicago for the Democratic Convention.

1.5: BURROUGHS AND WATTS' VISIT

Playboy offices.

Bob types furiously, occasionally stopping to chuckle at the brilliance of what he's just written. His desk buzzer sounds.

SECRETARY
(over intercom)

A Mr Alan Watts and his wife are here to see you.

WILSON

That's great. Send them up.

WATTS
(over intercom)

I've got this reprobate Bill Burroughs with me. Shall I bring him up too?

WILSON

William Burroughs? Absolutely.

He straightens himself up.

Watts, Burroughs and Jano arrive and exchange handshakes and hellos. Burroughs sits himself down and pulls out a piece of paper that he begins to study.

NB: In London we had a different notable actor/ personality play Burroughs each night.

JANO

Hello darling. Well everybody's come to Chicago – just like Abbie told us to.

WILSON

It's sure getting wild out there.

JANO

I hate to be a pain, but have you got some boards and markers darling? I want to make some placards for the protest.

WILSON

What time are we heading into the throng?

WATTS

Well we've got to get Bill here to the colosseum where he's delivering a speech.

BURROUGHS
(gesturing to the piece of paper he's studying)

Lyndon Johnson's un-birthday party.

> At times in the scene, Burroughs can be heard mumbling from his speech "The Purple Better One".

WILSON

Oh fantastic. Who else is speaking?

JANO

Terry Southern, Allen Ginsberg and Jean Genet.

WILSON

Oh wow.

BURROUGHS
(mumbling from his speech, under his breath)

Ladies and gentlemen, it is my coveted privilege and deep honour to introduce to you the distinguished senator and former Justice of the Supreme Court, Homer Mandrill, known to his friends as The Purple Better One.

JANO

So just time for a coffee and to make a few placards and then we should get our groove on.

WILSON

Sure.

(into intercom)

Donna, could you bring us some coffee, some big pens, paints and – large pieces of cardboard?

Jano nods.

DONNA
(over intercom)

Of course, Mr. Wilson.

                    WILSON
                (into intercom)
Thanks Donna.

                    WATTS
What are you working on, dear boy?

                    WILSON
Just a piece about what that eye in the pyramid on every dollar bill really means. It's a bit of Guerilla Ontology I'm engaged in.

                    WATTS
Extraordinary. I am just now reading the best book I've read in years. And it is called, *The Eye in the Triangle*.

                    WILSON
Wow.

                    JANO
Ah, it's the Net again.

                    WILSON
The Net?

                    JANO
The Net is like a web of coincidence that connects every-thing-in-the-universe with everything-else-in-the-universe.

                    WATTS
Dr John Lilly has whimsically suggested consciousness research activates the agents of

WATTS AND JANO
(in unison)

Cosmic Coincidence Control Centre!

> Donna, the bunny secretary enters carrying some boards and pens.

DONNA

Is this the kind of thing you meant, Mr Wilson?

WILSON

Jano?

JANO

Just perfect, my dear.

> With effortless sexiness, Donna places the cardboard and pens on the floor. Burroughs, Watts and Jano watch her go, enraptured.
>
> *NB: The part of Donna was performed in drag.*

WILSON

Like Jung's synchronicities?

JANO

What? Oh yeah, we're all living in Jungland, Bob. As we learn to consciously synchronise ourselves, we gain access to the territory of our totality. Yesterday they called it coincidence, today they call it synchronicity, tomorrow they will call it skill. Bill, tell Bob about your experiments with 23.

BURROUGHS

In the early 60s in Tangier I knew a certain Captain Clark who ran a ferry from Tangier to Spain. One day, Clark said to me that he'd been running the ferry for 23 years without an accident. That very day the ferry sank killing Clark and everybody aboard. That evening I was thinking about this when I turned on the radio.

The first newscast told me about a crash of an Eastern Airlines plane on the New York-Miami route. The pilot was also called Captain Clark and the flight was listed as Flight 23.

WILSON

"Captain Clark welcomes you aboard!"

BURROUGHS

So I began keeping records of odd coincidences. To my astonishment 23 appeared over and over again.

JANO

Oh yes, and many scientists agree with Carl Jung's opinion that the number of startling coincidences in the Net increase sharply around anybody who becomes involved in depth psychology or in any investigation that extends the perimeter of consciousness.

WILSON

I don't know. Maybe such people merely become more aware of coincidences.

> Burroughs shoots him a sharp look.

BURROUGHS

The dogma of science is that the will cannot possibly affect external forces. I think that's just ridiculous. It's as bad as the church. My viewpoint is the exact contrary of the scientific viewpoint.

WILSON

I'll start looking out for 23s.

JANO

All we know, Bob, is that the peculiar entities in charge of Cosmic Coincidence Control Centre pay special attention to those who pay attention to them.

WILSON

I like that.

WATTS

What's your angle on the eye-in-the-pyramid?

WILSON

I come up with a few. At the moment I'm rapping about the eye in the pyramid on the dollar bill. So many nation states have seen fit to festoon their currencies with magickal emblems: the Fleur de Lys, the Swastika, the Two Headed Eagle.

I'm trying to show how that symbolism is intrinsic to the whole monopolisation of psychic energy by the state. Here are two pieces of green paper; one is money, the other is not. The difference is that the former was blessed by the wizards in the treasury building.

BURROUGHS

Money is exactly the same as heroin in a capitalist society. A junkie must have regular doses, the capitalist citizen must have a regular money-fix. When junk becomes scarce, junkies behave desperately, and will steal or even kill. When money becomes scarce the capitalist citizens will also rob or kill.

WILSON

Yeah, because the state has co-opted the primate instinct for survival and replaced it with money, so that the neurochemistry of feeling safe, is hooked into an external power. The message, "money equals security, no money equals terror" is endlessly reinforced, until a token, the symbol money, controls our mental well-being.

BURROUGHS
(a glimmer of warmth)

And poverty doth make cowards of us all.

WILSON

So tell me more about this *Eye in the Triangle* book you were talking about.

WATTS

It's about Aleister Crowley.

WILSON

The British Satanist?

WATTS

Crowley certainly played the Satanist game on occasion, just as he played the Buddhist game, the Taoist game, the Hindu game, the atheist game and lots of others. It is emphatically not true that his reputation as Satanist and Black Magician was spread entirely by his enemies; he collaborated gleefully in blackening his own character.

WILSON

Why?

> Donna re-enters with the coffee, and makes a song and dance of pouring them all a cup.

WATTS

You don't understand the importance of terror. Most shamans are people who have gone through the death-rebirth process. Crowley knew, as many shamans do, that you can get this result quickly with some students by simply scaring the daylights out of them. A classic gimmick is to steadily increase their repressed suspicion that the beloved guru, in whom they have stupidly placed blind faith and love, is actually a diabolist out to destroy them, drive them mad or enslave them. Crowley used this technique often. The students who confront their fear and conquer it achieve a higher neurological awareness. How's that for your guerilla ontology?

WILSON

That works.

WATTS

Do have a look at Crowley, dear boy. He'll blow the top of your head off. *The Book of Lies* is the one. Crowley claimed that somewhere in that book he had revealed the inner secret of freemasonry and Illuminism, coded so that only those with "spiritual insight" would be able to decipher it.

WILSON

Now that's intriguing.

WATTS

Well quite. But it is *The Book of Lies*.

JANO

Right, I've done one for each of us. Bill, for you. Bob.

>   (to Alan)

One for you my darling. We need to get going.

>   WILSON

Once more unto the breach.

>   Shea enters

>   SHEA

Oh hi.

>   WILSON

This is Bob Shea. Bill, Jano and Alan Watts. You're joining us for the democratic convention aren't you?

>   SHEA

Am I?

>   JANO
>   (handing him a placard)

Oh look here's the one that went a bit wrong. I was trying something.

>   SHEA

Well Ok. I actually just popped in to say that Dr Timothy Leary has confirmed for your interview on Monday. He says he's looking forward to it.

>   WATTS

Oh Tim. Do send him my love.

>   BURROUGHS

Don't send him mine.

JANO

Oh Bill.

WILSON

You all know him?

WATTS

Oh yes. I last saw Tim when it was all going rather tits up at Harvard.

WILSON

Oh?

JANO

Tim never could contain himself – as far as he was concerned the procedures of scientific objectivity and rigor were simply an academic ritual designed to convince the university establishment that your work was dull and trivial enough to be considered "sound."

WATTS

It so happens that psychedelic chemicals make one curiously susceptible to pomposity.

SHEA

You've tried LSD?

They all nod

WATTS

Oh yes.

WILSON

And?

WATTS

My attitude to LSD is that when one has received the message, one should hang up the phone.

JANO

Come on, I don't want to be the one who's late for Jean. You know how he is.

> They drain their coffee cups and get up to leave.

BURROUGHS

One more thing about Crowley: He often referred to himself as Epopt of the Illuminati.

> MUSIC: That ding sound again. Another important connection.

> Footage of Chicago Riots/ Democratic convention with protest noise.

1.6: HOME FROM THE CONVENTION

> Wilson and Shea burst into Wilson's home, bent double, choking and groaning. Their eyes are streaming and they are clutching handkerchiefs to their faces.

SHEA

Man, that was a heavy scene.

WILSON

God, I hope the others got away OK. How are your eyes?

SHEA

Not good.

> Wilson fetches water and they begin to soak their eyes.

WILSON

I actually felt the moment my faith in the Democratic party died.

SHEA

Was it when the cops started chanting kill, kill, kill, or when they beat that kid repeatedly round the head? Or when they pulled out the teargas?

WILSON

Sat under that cross that the Concerned Clergymen had erected. I starting thinking they should have erected a tombstone instead. "Here lies the belief that all Evil is on the other side".

SHEA

Here lies American Liberalism.

WILSON

Yeah, clubbed to death by Chicago's heroic peace officers. You realise we're living in the embodiment of Discordian philosophy? Did you see the kids? They were all doing the Discordian hand signal. And they have no idea.

SHEA

We've unleashed some weird shit, no doubt about it.

> Wilson sits in his chair, and the desk lamp above his head turns on seemingly magically. The effect is a light bulb appearing above his head. They both laugh at the visual synchronicity.

SHEA

Ding! Whatever you say next will be the most important idea of both our lives.

> WILSON
> (pauses to think)

I think we should write The Great Discordian Epic American Novel.

> SHEA

I didn't know you were going to say that. Alright then. What will be the title?

> Wilson covers his eyes and runs his fingers along one of his bookshelves.

> WILSON

It's The History of Illuminism.

> SHEA
> (sarcastically)

What are the chances?

> WILSON

We shall call it – *Illuminatus*.

> SHEA

Ok! What's the opening line?

> WILSON
> (pauses to think for a moment)

"It was the year when they finally immanentized the Eschaton."

                            SHEA

Yes, yes. I like it.
                    (suddenly inspired)
It could begin with two detectives coming across those weird Illuminati memos that are all over your desk –

                            WILSON

– after their offices are mysteriously bombed.

>   A bomb explodes. When
>   the dust clears, what was
>   once the Playboy Office
>   has become the office of
>   *Confrontation Magazine* from
>   the *Illuminatus* book. Film
>   Noir-style music sets the tone
>   of the scene.

1.7: MULDOON AND GOODMAN

Two dirty rain macs and two trilby hats appear. With a flick of a collar and a puff on a cigar, Wilson and Shea become Muldoon and Goodman, two hard-bitten, fast-talking New York detectives.

GOODMAN (WILSON)

The office belongs to a magazine called Confrontation. It's kind of left-of-centre, so this was probably a right-wing job and not a left-wing one. The editor appears to have disappeared three days ago.

MULDOON (SHEA)

I think this is important. Damned important. I found it in the rubble, and it had been blown partly open, so I looked inside.

GOODMAN

And?

MULDOON

Freakiest bunch of interoffice memos I ever set eyes on. Weird as tits on a bishop.

GOODMAN

This is going to be a long night.

MULDOON

Illuminati Project memo:
JM: From the Encyclopedia Britannica: Illuminati, a short-lived movement of republican free-thought founded in 1776 by Adam Weishaupt. From 1778 onward they began to make contact with various Masonic lodges and often managed to gain a commanding position. The movement suffered from internal dissention and was ultimately banned by an edict of the Bavarian government in 1785.

GOODMAN

I'll make you a bet, Barney. The Joseph Malik who vanished is the JM these memos were written for.

MULDOON

Sure, these Illuminati characters are still around, and they got to him. Honest to God, Saul. I appreciate the way your mind usually pole-vaults ahead of the facts. But I say you're going too fast.

GOODMAN

Maybe I'm not going fast enough. An organisation that has existed for a couple of centuries minimum and kept its secrets pretty well hidden most of that time would be pretty strong by now.

MUSIC: Menacing

LUNA

Hello.

> Lights snap up. Luna has broken the spell. We're back in Wilson's living room.

WILSON
(a little caught out)

Oh hello, darling. This is Bob. Bob and I are going to write a book together.

LUNA

What kind of book?

WILSON

A big book.

LUNA

Bob and Bob's big book! Daddy, do you want an apple? Here catch.

As Wilson catches the apple, he and Shea look at each other discombobulated.

WILSON & SHEA

Hail Eris!

1.8: VISIT TO MILLBROOK

> Millbrook: an extravagant Georgian country house, with wrapping porch and turrets.
>
> Tripping hippies enter and paint each other's faces, blow bubbles and interact innocently with the audience.
>
> A white-coated doctor enters looking officious, and then it transpires that he is also tripping.
>
> A lover's tiff occurs just off stage, then Leary enters, still calling back.

LEARY

Go home, now, you're causing a scene. Christ do I have to fuck every girl who comes through here?

> He clocks Wilson and changes in an instant, flashing him a huge smile.

Mr. Wilson? Robert Anton Wilson?

WILSON

Please, call me Bob. Dr. Leary?

LEARY

Tim. Come on up, Bob. In fact let me come down. It's a beautiful day – do you play baseball?

> Leary joins Bob and they begin to walk the grounds.

So what do you want to know?

WILSON

Well firstly I guess I would like to know what scientific basis you have for the study of LSD?

LEARY

OK, Bob. The first thing you need to understand is that the psychedelic drug experience is a synergetic product of three factors: 1. The dosage of the chemical used; 2. The set – the subject's expectations, emotional status games, personality profile, etc; and 3. The setting – the actual events in space time.

> They come across a small group playing baseball.

LEARY

Take this baseball game, for example. What are the players actually doing in space-time? Who's at bat? Who's pitching? What are the rules of the game? How many strikes before you're out? Who makes the rules? Who can change the rules? These are the important questions, Bob. Anybody round here caught talking about "sickness" or "neurosis" or "ego" or "instinct" or any of that metaphysical jabberwocky gets thrown the hell out.

WILSON

OK, like the basic methodological position of post-Einstein physics. Nobody is sane or insane, right or wrong, hallucinating or not hallucinating. All that is just value judgements, relative to the observer's prejudices.

LEARY
(impressed)

Right. All that's happening in interpersonal relations is various parties or coalitions bargaining for control of neuro-muscular space –

> Shouts of annoyance from the baseball players as a tripped out young man picks up the ball and starts running, and a guy with a baseball bat chases him.

LEARY

OK, look. This guy thinks he's playing football. The other players think they're playing baseball so to them he's nuts. That's the battle happening all the time – the battle for the right to define the game for all other players.

WILSON
(Taking it in)

So you're really talking about using these drugs to change the whole personality? Ego and mind and emotions and all?

LEARY

Yes, Bob. That's the whole point. LSD with the right set and setting can change anything we consider ourselves. LSD takes you out of the normal space-time ego. I always go through a process in which the space game comes to an end, the time game comes to an end, and then the Timothy Leary game comes to an end. This is the peak, and at this point a new neurological imprint can be made, because all the old imprints are suspended for a while.

WILSON

But what about the dangers of brainwashing individuals against their will?

LEARY

Yep, it's the most potent brainwashing agent in the world. That's what my two commandments are all about. 1. Thou shalt not alter the consciousness of thy neighbour without his or her consent. 2. Thou shalt not prevent thy neighbour from altering his or her own consciousness.

WILSON

So how are the commandments going to be enforced, do you reckon?

LEARY

Number one, keep this out of the hands of the government. LSD will be abused and misused if they get control of this.

WILSON

So every individual should be allowed free access?

LEARY

No, God no. You mess with the set or the setting and you are going to end up with a lot of mind-rape, a lot of traumatized individuals. In my humble opinion it should be controlled and regulated by medical and psychological clinicians, according to a professional code of ethics.

WILSON

So how can I get some Doctor?

LEARY

Hahaha.

> Leary rummages through his pockets and hands him a dropper.

LEARY

The best results come when you fuck someone you really love, during the acid trip. That's when the nervous system is most open, most unconditioned, and ready to take a completely new imprint. Have fun, Bob.

1.9: BOB'S FIRST ACID TRIP

>Lights up on Wilson showing
>Arlen the tiny dropper bottle.

ARLEN
(incredulously)

No?

WILSON

Yes. Are the kids in bed?

ARLEN

Graham's out for the count. Karuna's staying over at the Walker's – don't roll your eyes. Luna's up. That child never sleeps.

WILSON

She's far too enlightened for sleep. You know what she told me the other day? She said she could see me glowing, but I had a black spot on my legs. Right where the polio gets me. Right where I had pain – she could literally see the pain.

ARLEN

Luna. That little angel.

                        WILSON

Oh and Alan Watts was telling me that I have to read some Aleister Crowley.

>   He pulls out *The Book of Lies*.

                        ARLEN

Who's that?

                        WILSON

He was a British Magician – sometimes known as The Beast. So I'm thinking perhaps LSD and Crowley is a good combination?

                        ARLEN

Sounds good.

                        WILSON

So, you want to come fly with me? Come fly, come fly away . . .

                        ARLEN

Oh shit! I'm supposed to be chairing the Women's Lib meeting. And besides, I'm not sure. You tell me what it's like and I might try it another time, OK?

>   Wilson sets the mood. He lights candles, lays out cushions, and dims the lights. Arlen pulls on her coat and searches for her bag.

                        ARLEN

You look like you're preparing to seduce someone.

WILSON

Timothy Leary said the setting is very important. So I'm trying to make it like it was when Luna was born.

ARLEN

Before that idiot doctor walked in and turned the lights on, just as she opened her little eyes.

WILSON

He also said it works best when you make love . . .

ARLEN

Another time. You have fun. And I won't turn the lights on when I walk in and make you cry. Happy rebirth.

>She leaves.

WILSON

In taking this sacrament, I wish to open myself without prejudice to a greater understanding of my life, the world around me and to a greater capacity for love. Now, did he say three drops or five?

> *NB: The audience often have an opinion about this and shout out. Wilson interacts with them freely.*
>
> Wilson drops the acid.
> He stares into the middle distance, holding a meditative pose. Long pause.

OK, so this is taking a little while.

> He relaxes.

So, what an interesting few days.

Aleister Crowley, possible Illuminati adept – LSD – and what was it Jano was going on about? The Net. Oh and Burroughs and his 23s. That was a weird story. And then that visit to the Death Convention – that's one I'll never forget. I'll include all that lot in *Illuminatus*.

> Behind him, in a rather wobbly fashion, Albert Hoffman rides past on his bicycle.

Is there anything to this 23 thing?

> He starts to pour over his books.

Hmm. This is taking a while. I might just do a little work on that Simon Moon scene.

> He begins to type, then Simon Moon emerges behind him.

MOON

Psst.

WILSON

Hello?

MOON

All Hail Discordia?

WILSON

Hail Eris.

MOON

Simon Moon. I heard you were coming up.

WILSON

Simon Moon?

MOON

Let's walk. I've got to get to the anarchists meeting.

> Wilson and Moon begin to pound the living room/streets of New York

WILSON

I was told I should ask you about the 23 enigma –

MOON

They're everywhere, man. 2 + 3 equals 5, the pentad within which the Devil can be invoked, while 2 divided by 3 equals 666. All the great anarchists died on the 23rd day of some month or other – Sacco and Vanzetti on August 23rd, Bonnie Parker and Clyde Barrow on May 23rd. Dutch on October 23rd. And Vince Coll was 23 years old when he was shot on 23rd St. JFK shot November 22nd and Oswald 24th – notice the conspicuous missing 23! Oh and Harpo Marx was born on November 23rd. You keep an eye out for the mystical 23 – you won't know what's hit you.

WILSON

It sounds like that way madness lies.

> Wilson tries to keep a distance from Moon, but Moon effortlessly keeps up with him, without skipping a beat.

MOON

Sanity? That's what you're after? Sanity? Listen, man. What the world calls sanity has led us to the present planetary crisis. Insanity is the only viable alternative.

WILSON

We all need to go insane to be liberated? I thought you believed in anarchism?

MOON

No. Anarchism remains tied to politics and is therefore a form of death like all other politics. That is until it breaks free from the defined "sanity" of capitalist society and creates its own reality. A pig for president, fucking in the streets.

>   Wilson finds this hilarious

Hoffman's discovery of LSD in 1943 was a manifestation of direct intervention by God in human affairs.

>   This blows Wilson's mind.

And we gotta get into tarot, man. Deep into tarot. Then we can fight the real enemy with their own weapons.

WILSON

So why are we walking to the anarchists meeting, then?

MOON

I'm booked to do a speech about all this.

WILSON
(giggling)

Well, I'm sure it'll go down a treat.

MOON

You don't dig it? I'm telling you man, the whole key to liberation is magic. Breaking up the trip that society has laid on us and starting our own trip.

WILSON

So you're talking about a kind of counter-conditioning?

MOON

Magic, counter-conditioning – the principle is the same. Bringing back realities that are supposed to be dead, Creating new realities. Astrology, demons, lifting poetry off the written page – and into the acts of your daily life. Surrealism, dig? Antonin Artaud and Andre Breton nailed it, man: "total transformation of mind, and all that resembles it".

> Wilson is now typing maniacally on an enormous typewriter. (The armchair flips to become this). He gets eaten and spat out by the typewriter, marking the intensification of the trip.

> *NB: In 2017 we used typewriter letter-cushions distributed on one bank of the four-sided audience to create the surreal typewriter.*

> Hoffman re-enters on his bicycle, and cycles around the stage.

WILSON

What are you looking for Hoffman?

HOFFMAN

I'm looking for my bicycle!

WILSON

Total transformation of mind and all that resembles it.

> Crowley appears in a puff of smoke.

CROWLEY

A man without a God is like a fish without a bicycle.

> MUSIC: Inquire Within

EVERYONE
(singing)

Inquire within! Inquire Within.
You never know what you might find.
Unscrew the inscrutable. Think the Unthinkable.
Dive down to the roots of your mind.
Inquire Within, Inquire Within.
Just don't believe all that you've seen.
Use your perception to answer the question:
Who is the master who makes the grass green?

> The room comes alive. Characters are hidden everywhere and now pop out to sing. Leary is an overturned basket of kid's toys, which turns into an enormous head-dress when lifted off the ground; Watts is hidden in a floor cushion and Burroughs appears from behind a shelf with a plant-pot on his head.

LEARY BASKET

The white man goes into his church and talks about Jesus. The shaman goes into his tipi, takes peyote and talks with Jesus.

WATTS FLOOR CUSHION

My dear man, reality is only a Rorschach ink-blot, you know.

PLANT POT

The father and the mother each provide 23 chromosomes.

LEARY BASKET

But forget ye not the Discordian Law of Fives. All incidents and events are directly connected to the number five, or to some multiple of the number five, or to some number related to five in one way or another . . .

LEARY AND WILSON

. . . given enough ingenuity on the part of the interpreter!

FLOOR CUSHION

You have achieved Discordian enlightenment when you realise that, while the goddess Eris and the Law of Fives are not literally true –

EVERYONE

Neither is anything else!

> A Pyramid rises up behind Wilson and from within it an enormous eye blinks and looks around.
>
> Hooded figures begin to emerge from it, forming a sinister circle around Wilson.

EVERYONE
(singing)

Inquire within! Inquire Within.
You never know what you might find.
Unscrew the inscrutable. Think the Unthinkable.
Dive down to the roots of your mind.
Inquire Within, Inquire Within.
Just don't believe all that you've seen
Use your perception to answer the question:
Who is the master who makes the grass green?

CROWLEY

Accidents have a way of happening to those who find out too much about the Bavarian Illuminati.

WILSON
(getting panicked)

What is the whole Illuminati enigma really about? What are you really trying to teach me?

ILLUMINATI

The final secret of the Illuminati is that you don't know you're a member until it's too late to get out.

> The Illuminati remove their hoods, becoming the crazed nuns of Wilson's Catholic upbringing.

NUNS

We've come to test your faith, sinner. Pour ground glass in to his eyes!

WILSON

No not my eyes!

> They crowd round him and force the glass into his eyes.

NUNS
(singing)

Inquire within! Inquire Within.
You never know what you might find.
Deranged and inscrutable. Proof irrefutable.
You've undone and broken your mind.

> The song ends.

CROWLEY

Never conjure what you can't put down.

> The nuns exit cackling, leaving Luna standing in her nightie, clutching a white rabbit cuddly toy.

LUNA

Daddy?

WILSON

They forced glass into my eyes.

LUNA

Let me see.

> He looks up and all the blood is gone.

LUNA

It's gone now, Daddy. I saw the witches leave.

WILSON

You saw them?

LUNA

They went out through the kitchen.

> The next exchange is very slow and deliberate.

WILSON

You are a baby ape.

LUNA

I'm a rat now. Now I'm a fish.

WILSON

You're a star!

LUNA

Molecular intelligence vibrating through time.

WILSON

Shiva and Kali, twin gods linked in an eternal dance. But Shiva is also Brahma and Jehovah and Pan!

LUNA

And Kali is also Nuit and Aphrodite and the Blessed Virgin Mary.

WILSON

The universe is the living embodiment of the divine couple, not a dead machine. I love you Luna.

LUNA

I love you too Daddy.

(pause)

The sadness is rising up now.

Wilson begins to sob.

WILSON

Why does the world have to be this way?

LUNA

How can you expect fairness and decency on a planet of sleeping people?

WILSON

How do we wake up?

> The room shifts back to normal lighting, and regular speed of speech. We are now seeing from Luna's point of view.

LUNA

Daddy, I don't know what you're talking about.

WILSON

You don't know what I'm talking about?

LUNA

I just want something to drink.

WILSON

Oh OK.

LUNA

I want some foot doot.

WILSON

Foot doot. Coming right up. I love that you still call it that.

LUNA

Foot doot, Daddy!

WILSON

Foot doot.

> Wilson pours a glass of orange juice, fascinated with every aspect of the process.

                    WILSON

Foot doot.

>   They share it in a solemn
>   ceremony, enjoying each sip
>   with wonder.

                    LUNA

I'm going back to bed.

                    WILSON

Will you stay down here with me?

                    LUNA

To keep you safe from the witches?

                    WILSON

You did see them?

                    LUNA

Daddy, you need a guardian angel.

                    WILSON

I've got one right here.

                              They snuggle up. Long
                              pause.

               STRANGE VOICE (V.O.)

What is more important than God?

                    EVERYONE

Nothing.

                  STRANGE VOICE

We shall look there then.

INTERVAL

ACT TWO

2.1: GATES OF ETERNITY

The Gates of Eternity once more. This time a bored angel waits at the threshold. A confused looking man in pyjamas makes his way through the audience and stands before the angel.

ANGEL

Go no further, O mortal, until you have proven to me your worthiness to enter paradise.

MAN

Just a minute, now. First of all, can you prove to me this is a real Heaven and not just the wishful fantasy of my disordered mind undergoing death?

> The Angel is lost for words.

VOICE FROM BEHIND CURTAIN

Let him in – he's one of us!

> A beat. Wilson emerges from behind the audience.
>
> As Wilson talks, Eris enters carrying make-up and a beard, and transforms Wilson into an old man.

WILSON

How you all getting on? You die-hard fans getting all het up about all the historical inaccuracies? Just think of them as Irish Facts. A bit like facts only better. So where are we in this rat's nest of a plot? Ah, yes. I've stumbled upon LSD, Discordianism and Aleister Crowley and Bob and I are well underway with our Magnum Opus, *Illuminatus*. And I knew in my gut that meeting Tim and Kerry and Bob was the kind of magickal initiation a man usually only dreams of. Life would never be the same again, as they say.

> Wilson is now an old man.

WILSON

What are you doing?

ERIS

You've got to be in 1994 in a moment.

WILSON

Which year am I in now?

ERIS

1977.

WILSON
(to audience)

Oh right. Where was I? It was all going so well, and then Tim Leary got arrested for possessing a joint and sentenced to 30 years in jail – and that kind of put a dampener on things.

LEARY
(from somewhere else)

A society that imprisons its philosophers is playing with very bad magick.

WILSON

You said it, Tim. And, as he also said, LSD is a drug that can bring about psychotic behavior in those who have NOT taken it.

(to Eris)

So will we be long in 1994?

ERIS

Oh for Goddess's sake, stop trying to work out which year we're in – it'll just blow your mind. Trust me.

                           WILSON

To the ends of the Earth.

                         (to audience)

Then, soon after the shock of learning that Leary had been arrested (and it really was a shock – for everyone), I received an urgent message from Ed Sanders, author of "Fuck God up the Ass" and other immortal works, warning: "There's nothing funny about the Illuminati. They're real." Of course I laughed immoderately, as the Fool always does before the doors of Chapel Perilous swing shut behind him.

                                   Eris shows Wilson his
                                   reflection in a small mirror.

                           WILSON

Oh boy, is this what I look like when I'm old?

                           ARLEN
                        (spinning round)

That's nothing. Look what they've done to me.

2.2: 1994

> Wilson is white-bearded and shaky, suffering with post-polio syndrome, but his eyes shine bright. He pops a hashish pill in to his mouth and goes back to his computer. He checks the time.

WILSON
(Shouting to Arlen, who is offstage)

Can you bring me the phone and the hospital number, Arlen? I need to call Bob.

> Arlen enters. She is now in her late 60s. She brings him the phone. He dials, shakily.

WILSON

Oh, yes, Can I speak to Robert Shea in ward 23 please?

(To Arlen)

I still can't get over it, he's in ward 23.

> (Shea comes to the phone)

To his bride said the keen-eyed detective
Can it be that my eyesight's defective?
Has the east tit the least bit
The best of the west tit
Or is that just a trick of perspective?

> Arlen exits, shaking her head.

WILSON

So how's your reality tunnel today, Bob? You sound pretty tired.

> (pause)

Yeah. So I've come up with a new principle. It's called the Cosmic Schmuck principle. If you never ask yourself if you are a Cosmic Schmuck then you, without any doubt, are a Cosmic Schmuck. The more you ask yourself if you are a Cosmic Schmuck, the less of a Cosmic Schmuck you become. Hey, you see NYPD Blue? "This'll rock your socks, John, but I gotta tell you: occasionally we don't achieve perfect justice in this building".

> (pause)

OK, what about: "once or twice a year I like to keep a promise to a witness so I remember what it feels like."

> (pause)

Yeah, he gets all the best lines, alright. OK Bob. I won't tire you out any more. I love you too.

> (pause)

> He hangs up the phone.

WILSON

(To Arlen, he thinks, but she's out of the room)

Why is it that in this society it takes three decades and a major illness before two heterosexual males can say "I love you" to each other?

ARLEN (OS)

I can't hear you!

> The phone rings, but before he can answer it, Arlen has answered it in another room.

Hello? What do you mean? Yes, I've got it right here. Oh Jesus Christ. Alright, thanks Melissa.

> Arlen walks in and dumps the Los Angeles Times in Wilson's lap.

WILSON
(reading)

"Noted science-fiction author Robert Anton Wilson was found dead in his home yesterday, apparently the victim of a heart attack. Mr Wilson, 63, was discovered by his wife, Arlen. He was the author of numerous books, most notably *The Illuminatus Trilogy* which he co-wrote with Robert Shea. He was noted for his libertarian viewpoints, love of technology and off-the-wall humor. Mr Wilson is survived by his wife and two children."

ARLEN

The guy who started this has gotten dangerously close to black magic.

WILSON

Science fiction author? Only six of my books could be called science fiction.

ARLEN

That's what you're worried about?

WILSON

Love of technology? Is that the best they could come up with? Love of technology.

ARLEN

I better phone the kids before they see this crap.

> She exits. Wilson logs on to his computer and starts to read all the messages.

WILSON

"The CIA killed Robert Anton Wilson. Wilson did not die of natural causes. He was assassinated. Earlier today Wilson was injected with a time-delay poison based on shellfish toxin, by agents of the CIA's special Super Secret Black Operations Squad, using a special microscopic needle made of a plastic which dissolves in the body . . ." Oh, this is cute as a shit house rat.

> He goes on reading. Arlen comes back in.

ARLEN

OK, Graham had heard something but didn't believe it. It's the first Karuna had heard, but she is seriously pissed off about it.

WILSON

My God, Arlen. Reading this you'd think that my works belong alongside Homer, and by all accounts my soul ranks in the vicinity of Buddha and Saint Teresa of Avilla.

> The phone rings again. Arlen answers, exiting as she talks.

ARLEN

Fly Agaric, hi. No it's not true. He's absolutely fine . . .

> Wilson goes on reading.

WILSON

"This is as bad as learning that Zappa died. Now let's get out there and party like he'd want you to!"

> Arlen comes back in.

ARLEN

... OK. Please let people know. Alright, thanks for calling, Fly.

WILSON

You know, Arlen, maybe I am dead. Like that Philip K Dick book when all the dead people don't know they've died and just think the universe is slowly turning to shit. *Ubik*.

ARLEN

You just sit here on the sofa laughing about it all and I'll take an endless stream of phone calls from your distraught friends and admirers shall I?

WILSON

Arlen, you are the greatest woman a man could wish for. And so beautiful.

ARLEN

Oh, that's just my soul you're looking at.

WILSON

Tell them the Illuminati did it.

ARLEN

Half of them already think that.

WILSON

I have become Schrodinger's cat!

> The phone rings again.

WILSON

Whoever that is, break it to them gently – the news of my continuing existence, or at least my continuing delusion of existence.

ARLEN

Hello? Oh hi Tim. No, it's all bullshit. He's right here in front of me – and I know he's not dead because he's annoying the crap out of me. It's Tim Leary. You talk to him.

WILSON

Oh hi Tim. I seem to be living inside a Robert Anton Wilson novel. Apparently I've been assassinated by the CIA. And you're implicated. Did you see this? "Earlier the CIA had LSD advocate Timothy Leary neutralised with a neurotoxin which artificially induces a state similar to senility . . ." So if you try to tell people I'm alive, that is just further evidence of your senility! I know, it explains a lot! And wow – Fly Agaric has posted something already: "I have contacted Wilson's wife and she tells me he's alive. But I'm pretty gullible."

ARLEN

Oh, for God's sake.

WILSON

OK, Tim. Yeah you go and spread your senile ramblings. I'll speak to you soon. Assuming I am indeed alive.

ARLEN

You are enjoying this way too much.

WILSON

My God, I just feel bad that I haven't actually done my bit to earn all these incredible eulogies. It's actually totally overwhelming.

The phone rings again.

                    ARLEN

Hello?

>   Arlen's face goes white, but
>   Wilson is enjoying reading
>   his eulogies too much to
>   notice.

Ok. I'll tell him. Thanks Rose. I'll tell him.

                    WILSON

I love this one: "There is no toxin. There is no needle. You have not heard of a toxin. You have not heard of a needle. There is no conspiracy. Fnord. Repeat after me. Fnord. There is no toxin."

                    ARLEN

Bob? Bob? Bob is dead.

                    WILSON

Don't tell me you believe it too . . .

                    ARLEN

Robert, Bob. Robert Shea is dead.

>   Wilson stops, shocked.
>   He steps back into the old
>   Playboy offices where his
>   friend, alive and well, is
>   typing furiously.

2.3: PLAYBOY OFFICES

Playboy offices – 1969

SHEA

Did you get the next *Illuminatus* chapter?

WILSON

Bob, it's brilliant. George Dorn's jailbreak is just hilarious. With cum on his trousers! And Mavis, wow – what a woman.

SHEA

Yes, I kind of picture George Dorn like Greg Hill.

WILSON

OK, so – I've got a great character. He lives on a yellow submarine that he's designed himself that's completely undetectable. A free-floating utopia. I think he's called Hagbard Celine.

SHEA

Yes, I like it! He could be the leader of the Discordians.

WILSON

Great. And he could talk to Dolphins like John Lilly.

SHEA

Yeah, and visit Atlantis.

WILSON

Ok wow. Yeah. Alright. I'll get to work on him. And we need to get the Democratic Convention in there –

SHEA

God, yeah. The day the dream died.

WILSON

Or we all woke up just a little bit more.

SHEA

Bob, you realise that when I met you I still thought abortion was immoral, the government had our best interests at heart and there was no such thing as a gay priest.

WILSON

You've come a long way, Robert Joseph Shea. You ever think it's time to take the leap into being a full-time writer?

SHEA

Give up a job, this sweet? As we feared: writing this book is unhinging your mind.

WILSON

I don't know. I think remaining in the same job, the same town, the same belief-system, year after year, has the effect of gradually narrowing your tunnel of reality. Perhaps the way to stay young is to make a quantum jump every so often and land yourself in a new reality-matrix.

SHEA

Bob, not when you're on 20,000 per!

WILSON

(laughing, but tinged with sadness)

OK, perhaps not.

SHEA

Listen, how are we doing with the *Playboy* letters?

WILSON

I did all that – don't worry. We've got the whole week to sail the seven seas with Hagbard Celine and his merry band of Discordians. I keep picturing Hagbard as Tim Leary. Listen to this:

Wilson reads aloud as he types, then the speech is taken over by Timothy Leary who is dressed in outrageous futuristic clothing. He is now in fact the fictional character, Hagbard Celine.

The following scene is enacted in high-camp style, with crazy scenery and lots of extras.

LEARY/HAGBARD CELINE

Welcome to the tribe. My name is Hagbard Celine. We want to recruit you, because you are so gullible. That is, gullible in the right way. You're sceptical about conventional wisdom, but attracted to unorthodox ideas. An unfailing mark of Homo Neophilus.

GEORGE

Home-Neophilus?

HAGBARD/WILSON

The human race is not divided into the irrational and the rational, as some idealists think. All humans are irrational, but there are two different kinds of irrationality – Neophobus who reject new ideas and embrace what they have known all their lives and Neophilus who love new things, invention, innovation, change. Neophobus is the original human stock. Neophilus is the creative mutation that has been popping up at regular intervals during the past million years. They live life the way it should be lived: ninety-nine per cent mistakes and one per cent viable mutations. Everyone in my organisation is neophilus, George. That's why we're so far ahead of the rest of the human race. Concentrated Neophilus influences without any Neophobe dilution. We make a million mistakes, but we move so fast that none of them catch up with us –

GEORGE

Where the hell did you get this ship? I wouldn't have believed a submarine like this could exist without the whole world knowing about it.

HAGBARD

The sub's my creation, built in accordance with my design in a Norwegian fjord. This is what the liberated mind can do. I am the twentieth-century Leonardo, except that I'm not gay. I've tried it, of course, but women interest me more. The world has never heard of Hagbard Celine. That is because the world is stupid and Celine is very smart.

Have you met FUCKUP?

GEORGE

No?

HAGBARD

First Universal Cybernetic-Kinetic-Ultramicro-Programmer. I'll put it to holographic mode. It's real claim to uniqueness is a programmed stochastic process whereby it can throw an I Ching Hexagram, crosscheck with current scannings of today's political, economical, meteorological, astrological, astronomical and technological eccentricities and provide a reading combining the best of scientific and occult methods.

GEORGE

Er, pleased to meet you.

HAGBARD

Right. FUCKUP, throw today's I Ching.

> FUCKUP whirrs to life and blows a load of balls everywhere.

FUCKUP

I'll put it to holographic mode.

MAVIS & CREW GIRL

Oo-oo

HAGBARD

Based on the image of a future mage, so it tells me. But that's all tricks.

> *NB: Our FUCKUP was played by a digitally-enhanced version of Alan Moore.*

FUCKUP

Today, April 23rd, the stochastic pattern spontaneously generated is Hexagram 23, "Breaking Apart".

HAGBARD

Hmm. Always a strong one, this.

FUCKUP

The breaking apart is fundamentally the schizoid and schismatic mental fugue of lawyer-politicians attempting to administrate a worldwide technology whose mechanisms they lack the education to comprehend and whose gestalt-trend they frustrate by breaking apart into obsolete Renaissance nation-states.

> Outside the porthole appears a swimming dolphin.

GEORGE

Who's that?

HAGBARD

That's Howard.

HOWARD
(singing)

The foe is attacking, their ships coming near, Now is the time to attack without fear!

MAVIS

The Illuminati! They're here!

HOWARD
(singing)

Illuminati Illuminati – come to break up your Discordian party

HAGBARD
(corpsing)

Button up your asshole, George. We're in for a fight.

HAGBARD

Battle stations – everyone. Now!

> Sirens blare and lights flash. Discordians appear on lower gantry. Torpedoes are passed around in preparation for battle.
>
> An overlong pause as everyone seems to be waiting for something to happen.

Sorry, line?

                    KEN CAMPBELL
               (standing up from the audience)

Oh for Christ's Sake.

                              The whole scene goes limp.

                    HAGBARD ACTOR

Sorry, Ken. It'll be alright on the night.

                         KEN

Alright on the night? Alright on the night? We might all be dead by the fucking night. I want to have fun now!

                              He points to the chap playing
                              George Dorn.

And you! You are the plug-hole of this entire production. Everything that is great about it is disappearing down you.

> Ken steps out of the audience and onto the stage.

Alright re-set the balls. And go and learn your fucking lines. I've got to talk to this filmmaker chap.

> HAGBARD ACTOR
> (to another actor)

I don't know what I'm talking about half the time.

> The actors come off stage, talking in English accents, they re-set the stage, paint sets, try on costumes etc.

> KEN

Right, I haven't got long. I'm just slinging on an 11 hour epic with no money. What do you want to know?

> FILMMAKER

Well, I suppose – er – how you came to be putting on this production?

> KEN

I get this phone call from a Liverpudlian poet chap, Peter O'Halligan, to say he's been reading Carl Jung's book *Memories, Dreams and Reflections* and on page 223 he – Jung– talks about this dream he's had about Liverpool being the pool of life. There's a little fountain and whatnot. Anyway Jung reckons this is his most important dream.

So this poet chap, O'Halligan, makes it his commission to find the exact spot of Jung's dream. So he's phoning me to say that he's found it. It's on the corner of Mathew St, right near the Cavern Club where the Beatles first performed.

Anyway the building on the corner of this most holy spot turns out to be derelict, so O'Halligan claims it. He's telling me that he's set up a caff in the basement and he wants to know if I'll come and stick something on for him. He's called it The Liverpool School of Language, Music, Dream and Pun.

So I pop along to Compendium book shop to scout out some possible ideas for this show, and I pick up a few fairly interesting looking bits and pieces, and then I come across this book with an enormous Yellow Submarine on the front. So there's the Beatles connection. It's called *Illuminatus* by a couple of *Playboy* editors called Robert Anton Wilson and Robert Shea. And it's the greatest book on Planet World.

But I didn't know that at this point. So I decide to test it. I thought right: Jung's dream was on page 223 of *Memories, Dreams and Reflections* so I'll turn to page 223 of this submarine book and if it's interesting, I'll sling on a production of that. So I turn to page 223 and who should be mentioned, but Carl Gustav Jung?!

Yeah. That stopped me in my tracks. So I phone back Peter O'Halligan and say "Yeah Peter I've got the show for you. And we're going to be called The Science Fiction Theatre of Liverpool.

So here we all are staging the Greatest Show on Planet World in a cafe squat in the Pool of Life on the site of Jung's most important dream.

Sean over there was a bit put out at first because he lives in the corner of this floor. But he's on board now, and he's knocking out a wall and turning his flat into the royal box, isn't that right, Sean?

SEAN

Yes Ken.

> The filmmaker cuts.

FILMMAKER

That's great, Ken.

KEN

So how did you come to be making a film about us in your cardigan?

FILMMAKER
(flustered)

Well urm. I heard about it from a friend back in London.

KEN

Who?

FILMMAKER

Urm Brian Gilbert

KEN

Oh that burk. Yes?

FILMMAKER

Yes, and well I put in an application to the arts council and got the go ahead.

> The cast winces as the filmmaker says this

KEN

You got funding from the arts council?

                    FILMMAKER

Yes.

                    KEN

They won't fund the greatest show on Planet World, but they'll fund some prick who's heard about it from his burky mate in a pub?

                    The filmmaker is laughing
                    along nervously

                    HAGBARD ACTOR
            (to himself, cowering and covering his eyes)

Oh God, don't laugh you stupid fucker.

                    KEN

You think I'm joking? You know what funded is don't you? Fun Dead. You and your arts council funded camera are sucking the fun out of the true geniuses. Fun Dead. A conspiracy of mediocrity. Go on you can fuck off and tell that Brian burk not to send any more pillocks up to Liverpool. Go on, fuck off out of here.

                    The filmmaker realises he's
                    deadly serious and bundles
                    his stuff and himself out of
                    there.

                    FILMMAKER
                (from a safe distance)

Fine, Ken. You carry on up your own arsehole.

                    KEN
              (chasing him)

Yes, I fucking well will. And I'll find the whole secret of the Great Cosmic Joke up there, right up inside my arsehole – and you can crawl to the arts council to see if they'll fund you to come in and have a look . . .

                    Filmmaker exits

              (to the actors)

Right let's do the end of the George Dorn Initiation.

                BILL DRUMMOND

I can't get this set right, Ken.

                    KEN

Just ask yourself one question, Bill. Is it heroic?

                BILL DRUMMOND

Also Ken, are we referring to the Submarine folk as Discordians or the Justified Ancients of Mu Mu?

                    KEN

Discordians.

                BILL DRUMMOND
              (under his breath)

Yeah, that's a mistake.

                          Chris, the actor playing
                          George Dorn (same as Greg
                          Hill) gets up to fuck an
                          enormous Golden Apple.

KEN

Come on Chris get your kit off. We've still got the Black Mass scene to get to.

(to someone offstage)

Did we settle on who's doing the cunnilingus?

HAGBARD

Are ye a human being and not a cabbage or something?

DORN

Yes.

HAGBARD

That's too bad. Do you wish to better yourself?

DORN

Yes.

KEN

Really fuck that apple all over the place will you, Chris? I want to see your bouncing buttocks.

HAGBARD

How stupid. Are ye willing to become philosophically illuminated?

DORN

Yes.

HAGBARD

Very funny. Will ye dedicate yourself to the Erisian movement?

KEN

Camper Hagbard. This is far too important to take seriously.

DORN

Probably.

HAGBARD

Then repeat after me: Before the Goddess Eris, I George Dorn do hereby declare myself a brother of the Legion of Dynamic Discord.

KEN

That's it chase him all over the place!

DORN

Before the Goddess Eris, I George Dorn do hereby declare myself a brother of the Legion of Dynamic Discord.

> Ken chases Dorn, spanking him. Dorn fucks the apple with increasing vigor and abandon.

KEN

Come on climax then.

HAGBARD

Hail Eris! All hail Discordia!

> Dorn climaxes desperately.

KEN

Now that's what I call theatre.

HAGBARD ACTOR

It was never like this at the Royal Shakespeare Company.

KERRY enters.

WILSON
(shouting over the actor's hubbub to Ken)

What's going on – who is this character now?

KEN

That's Kerry Thornley. It's not *Illuminatus* rehearsals in Liverpool any more. He's popping off for a quick scene in 1950s New Orleans for some reason – I'm sure it'll become clear later on.

WILSON

And who are you?

KEN

I'm Ken Campbell. Big fan.

WILSON

Pan?

KEN

Fan. In about 9 years time I'll be putting on a stage version of that *Illuminatus* book you're writing back in 1969.

WILSON

Oh. Confusing.

KEN

Hail Eris! Anyway – New Orleans, 1957.

2.4: NEW ORLEANS — 1957

> Ken is handed a hat and a cigar and turns seamlessly into Gary Kirstein. He sits at a café table, sipping whiskey and coolly smoking his cigar. A landscape painting is propped on a small easel.
>
> Slim Brooks enters with a young Kerry Thornley.

SLIM

Kerry, this is Gary. Gary, this is Kerry. He don't like Kennedy either.

GARY
(nasal Midwestern twang)

John F. Kennedy is a menace to the country and he ought to be assassinated.

KERRY

At last, somebody in the French Quarter who isn't a Liberal!

GARY

Not only that, but I'm a Nazi and, actually, we won the war, Kerry. Did you know that?

> Gary laughs, eyes unsmiling. Kerry laughs along, innocently.

GARY

Thank you, Slim. We'll be alright.

> Slim exits.

KERRY

I like that painting.

GARY

I did that.

KERRY

You're a good painter.

GARY

So was Hitler. In fact an art critic once complained that you could count the number of cobblestones in one of his street scenes. I don't think that was a very fair criticism. Do you, Kerry?

KERRY

I should say not. We Objectivists like realistic art that requires genuine talent. That critic was probably an abstract expressionist or something equally decadent.

GARY

Precisely. Kerry, how would you like to be famous?

KERRY

I'd love it. I've always wanted to be at least famous enough to make the cover of *Time* magazine.

GARY
(Suddenly very serious, hunching forward)

I can make you famous. In order to make you famous I'll have to kill five people.

KERRY

Sure. Go ahead.

GARY

Kerry, if one man saves the life of another man, would you agree with the notion that the first man then has the right to do whatever he wants with the life of the man he has saved?

KERRY

I don't know, but I read that the Chinese believe that if you save another man's life, then from that day forward you are to blame for any crimes he commits.

GARY

Answer my question, Kerry. Does the man who saves the life have the right to do whatever he wants with the life he has saved? Or not?

KERRY

Yeah, I guess so –

GARY

Well, OK then. I'm writing a book entitled, *Hitler Was A Good Guy*. That's a working title. The secret to

Hitler's power was that he had no power. He was instead surrounded by powerful men – and they trusted him only because he had no power of his own. And that's why he was powerful.

KERRY

I've written a book.

GARY

Oh yes?

> Kerry wrestles his bag to see if he has a copy. He does.

KERRY

It's about this guy I was in the marines with. After we'd been in Japan together he one day just gets up and defects to Russia.

GARY

What was your pal's name?

KERRY

Lee Harvey Oswald. I haven't heard from him since. Guess he's still out there. I've called it *The Idle Warriors*.

GARY

I'd like to take a look at that book some time.

KERRY

I have a copy right here.

> He hands it to Gary.

So you're a writer, eh, Kerry?

KERRY

Yes Sir.

GARY

So I guess you're in need of a few bucks then.

KERRY

Always.

GARY

Will you do some research for me, Kerry? Go to the library and research all the ways that the other top Nazis were actually worse than Hitler. Write it all out for me. Be sure to put the working title at the top of each page: "Hitler was a good guy". I'll give you a buck a page.

KERRY

Alright.

GARY

So how we gonna kill that son of a bitch Kennedy, then?

KERRY
(laughing)

Remote control plane with a bomb on board?

GARY

I think the best way to pull off a political assassination – *and get away with it* – would be to have many people involved, but kept under the illusion that they were pursuing other goals.

KERRY

I heard it said that the only strategy an opponent cannot predict is a random strategy. You could call it Operation Mindfuck.

GARY

You could indeed.

KERRY

If I were to assassinate someone, afterwards I'd have myself hypnotised so that I'd forget all about it.

Gary nods, smiling.

GARY

Only one problem remains: who to frame? I figure some jailbird.

KERRY

Why?

GARY

Because people who are caught for crimes are weak.

KERRY

Well personally I think a communist would make a better patsy.

Gary nods again thoughtfully.

GARY

Now you get those pages along to me and I'll give you your money, alright, Kid?

                         KERRY

Alright.

                              With his hands in his pockets,
                              whistling, Kerry unwittingly
                              walks through Chapel
                              Perilous. Creepy music.

                    GARY
              (picking up Kerry's book)
Lee Harvey Oswald, hmm . . .

2.5: ARRIVING AT THE NEW HOUSE

The Wilson family are laden with bags, making their way along a dusty hot road to their new home.

KARUNA

Oh my God, we're in the middle of nowhere. Why are we moving to this hovel?

ARLEN

You know why. So your father can be a full-time writer and I can do my poetry and you guys can play outside.

KARUNA

But New Mexico? Did we have to move so far away from – everything?

LUNA

I think it's an adventure. I'm feeling good vibes.

KARUNA

But if dad's not at *Playboy* anymore, how are we going to have any money?

> Arlen and Wilson exchange worried looks.

GRAHAM

It's not all about money.

> Laughter at this precocious statement.
>
> They trudge on.

GRAHAM

When do we get there? I'm bored.

LUNA

Why don't we do Mum's poem to pass the time?

ARLEN

Again, really? OK, but only if we get it right this time.

ALL TOGETHER (SUNG AS A ROUND)

This is the world that man made.
These are the ills that plagued
The world that man made.
Man made, man made, man made
This is the doctor prescribing the pills
That treated the ills that plagued
The world that man made
Man made, man made, man made
These are the plants and labs and mills
That manufactured all the pills the doctor
Gave to treat the ills that plagued
The world that man made
Man made, man made, man made
This is the banker with tellers and tills

That backed the plants and labs and mills
That manufactured all the pills the doctor
Gave to treat the ills that plagued
The world that man made
Man made, man made, man made
This is the general with trumpets and trills
Who made the war that saved the bank that
Backed the plants that manufactured all the pills
The doctor gave to treat the ills that plagued
The world that man made
Man made, man made, man made
Here is the mother all forlorn
Whose one and only child was born
To die in the war the general made to save
The bank that backed the plants that made
The pills the doctor gave to treat the ills
That plagued the world that man made
Man made, man made, man made
This is the angel that blew his horn
To comfort the mother all forlorn
And fired the general and closed the banks
And shut the mills and scattered the pills,
Retired the doctor and cured the ills
And ended the world that man made –

> They arrive at the new home.
> It's in a dreadful state.
>
> There's a moment of disappointment as they take in the degree of dilapidation.

LUNA

I think it's a magic house.

                     WILSON

I think you're a magic girl.

                     ARLEN
                  (she's lost him)

Graham!

                    KARUNA
                  (as she exits)

You realise my life is now basically over?

2.6: BOB'S BIRTHDAY MORNING

> Wilson is reading in bed.
> Arlen is asleep next to him.

WILSON
(to audience)

Over the next few months I continued to seriously experiment with Crowley's techniques for mutating consciousness. The first results of the various Crowleyan experiments were a vast increase in my already abundant scepticism – to the point where I was at least sceptical about scepticism itself.

> Wilson picks up *The Book of Lies*. Slowly Arlen wakes up.

ARLEN

Happy birthday, my darling.

> They kiss.

You're reading that again?

WILSON

It's the book that Crowley said those with sufficient spiritual insight could find the –

ARLEN

I know, I know. The secret to freemasonry and Illuminism.

WILSON

Am I that boring and predictable?

> He bites his thumb, hard.
> Whelps.

ARLEN

What are you doing?

WILSON

It's one of Crowley's experiments: The thumb must be bitten very hard, if this entity you're talking to utters the word . . . "I".

> He bites himself again.

WILSON

In fact, Crowley used to slash at his wrist with a razor, but that seemed a bit . . .

WILSON & ARLEN

. . . extreme . . .

> He goes back to reading for some time.

ARLEN

So, you've read it like a hundred times . . . and?

WILSON

I don't have sufficient spiritual insight.

ARLEN

You just said I.

WILSON

Shit.

> He bites himself again, hard.
> Then has a revelation.

WILSON

Wait a minute. The way to succeed. The way to succeed! And of course –chapter 69. The way to succeed!

ARLEN

What? *What?*

WILSON

The way to suck seed. Look and here – the way to success – suck ess – suck eggs. The chapter number is usually related to the subject of the chapter but normally it's cabalistic – that had thrown me off track. But it's simple: 69 – the way to suck seed and suck eggs! And look here "the descent of the dove on Pentecost is called The Gift of Tongues . . .

ARLEN

So . . .

WILSON

He's saying that mutual oral sex is the secret behind freemasonry and Illuminism.

ARLEN

Really?

WILSON

And – that makes sense of that passage about– Yes!

(Reading)

"I have sacrificed a male child of perfect innocence and high intelligence 150 times every year since 1912." He means the sacrifice is his semen – a male child – and within the DNA code it does contain a very high intelligence, the genetic blueprint of planet Earth!

ARLEN

69ers are the secret of the Illuminati?

WILSON

Well, probably sexual yoga – tantra – in general.

(getting excited)

They're not a fantasy of right-wing paranoids. The Illuminati is one of the names of an underground mystical movement using sexual yoga.

ARLEN

Well, I guess that explains the secrecy.

WILSON

Yes! There's always a veil of obscurity and mystery around these occult figures – Bruno, John Dee, Cagliostro – Crowley himself– which paranoids assume is to do with plots to take over the world – but more likely it was a screen to protect them from persecution from various holy inquisitions.

Wow – I

(bites thumb)

This collection of molecules you call your husband, thought he'd never figure that one out. Chapter 69 – it seems so obvious now. My fault for not having a dirty enough mind.

ARLEN

Oh it's pretty dirty when it wants to be.

WILSON

Yes, we may have some experimenting to do in this area.

> He begins to disappear under the sheets as Arlen lies back.
>
> Then Graham runs in.

GRAHAM

I just met a silver space lady who told me I have to become a fizzysist when I'm older.

ARLEN

Wow!

> Graham runs out. Luna enters

LUNA

Happy birthday dad.

WILSON

Thanks Angel. Did Graham just meet somebody?

LUNA

Yeah, the same silvery people we saw with the spaceship.

WILSON

Or helicopter or whatever it was.

LUNA

He's so happy. But he didn't know what a physicist was.

WILSON

He came and told you that a silver woman had informed him he had to be a physicist and he didn't know what it meant?

LUNA

That's cool isn't it?

Karuna enters.

KARUNA

Happy birthday, dad.

WILSON

Thanks sweetheart.

KARUNA

I've done a little reading and today is a special day for you guys. The sun is in Capricorn which is your sign, Dad, and the moon is in Cancer, which is your sign Mum. So it's going to be an interesting day . . . And a good day for lurve . . ..

ARLEN

Yes, thanks Karuna

WILSON

You know I don't buy astrology.

ARLEN

I.

Wilson bites his thumb.

ARLEN

This thing is going to annoy me.

KARUNA
(to Wilson)

Because you're closed-minded.

WILSON

Oh, like Luna levitating the other day?

KARUNA

I'm telling you. We were both meditating and when we started she was on the left of me. When we finished she was on the right.

LUNA

Dad, you believe in ESP so it happens around you. You don't believe in levitation so it doesn't happen around you.

Luna exits

KARUNA

Closed minded.

WILSON

Scientifically minded. Alright. A record will be kept of anything significant that occurs today. Scientifically. But the man in this bed does worry about you kids believing any crazy new-age theory that comes your way.

KARUNA

Why are you talking weird?

ARLEN

Your father can't say the word I.

KARUNA

You call us weird.

LUNA (VO)

Mum can you come please?

ARLEN

What's up sweetie?

LUNA

I've just started my period.

WILSON

My little Luna is a woman.

KARUNA

Put that in your notebook.

LUNA (VO)

Mum!

ARLEN
(jumping out of bed)

I'm coming.

KARUNA

Are we going out for your birthday? Or are we too poor to even do that?

WILSON
(sighing)

We're going to meet up with Jules and the gang for lunch. Then you're all going to stay at theirs.

Karuna begins to exit

Turn on the radio for me please, will you Karuna.

                    Karuna turns the radio on.

KARUNA

Yes, father. Oh masterful one.

                    Smooth, jazzy music plays.
                    Karuna exits.

WILSON

The way to Suck Seed. Hahaha. Only for those with Spiritual Insight. You old goat, Aleister. This does begin to shed a very different light on the Illuminati and what they were up to.

ARLEN (V.O.)
(she hasn't heard properly)

What's that?

WILSON

The Illuminati were perhaps more like an order of initiated Adepts whose work is to initiate and illuminate mankind.

ARLEN (V.O.)

Can't hear you!

WILSON
(shouting)

Initiated adepts! – Oh never mind.

RADIO

"America's most wanted man, LSD advocate Timothy Leary has been arrested in Afghanistan by American agents."

WILSON
(shocked)

Oh, Tim.

ARLEN
(entering)

What's happened?

WILSON

He's been kidnapped.

LUNA (VO)

Mum! I need help.

WILSON

The blood of the lamb.

KARUNA
(entering)

Who's been kidnapped?

WILSON

Tim Leary. He'd been a free man for two years since escaping. Now they'll lock him up and throw away the key.

KARUNA

And put that in your notebook.

Karuna exits. Graham enters.

GRAHAM

What is a fissyzist again?

ARLEN
(end of tether)

OK kids out. Go on. Go and make Dad a lovely birthday breakfast.

Kids exit.

WILSON

God, I didn't realise how much I care for Tim.

ARLEN

For someone so brilliant, he can be so incautious. They'll put him in maximum security now. He'll probably commit suicide within a year.

Pause. Wilson suddenly sits upright.

WILSON

I – I – Oh –

(bites thumb)

My Mystic just had a really clear vision – a flash of Tim grinning.

ARLEN

I just don't see how he can make it through this.

WILSON

No, honestly. My Mystic saw with that total inner certainty.

ARLEN

How do you mean?

                    WILSON

It's occurred a few times since the experiments began. It's as real as knowing you're about to vomit or ejaculate. You can't mistake it.

                    ARLEN

And what did you see?

                    WILSON

The Mystic says that the very first photo we'll see he'll have the old Leary grin flashing again.

                    ARLEN

Well, I really hope you're right.

                    WILSON

I am. In handcuffs but grinning. I saw it.

                                        They exit the bedroom.

                    ARLEN (V.O)

I.

                    WILSON (V.O.)

Ouch.

                              ***

                              A burst of jazzy music indicates some time is passing.

                              Arlen and Wilson return to the bedroom. It is now night time.

WILSON
(to audience)

A few hours later we drove into a pizza parlour in Mendocino to celebrate my birthday. On the way we bought a newspaper. There on page one was Leary in handcuffs. And –

ARLEN
(also to audience, with a bemused shrug)

He was grinning.

WILSON

I think I owe Karuna an apology about my astrology scepticism. A more significant day I'd be hard-pressed to find.

ARLEN

And now the whole of tonight and tomorrow to ourselves with no children. A good day for lurve.

WILSON

To discover a little more about the secrets of the Illuminati. What was it –the gift of tongues?

ARLEN

That's right. Sounds fun.

WILSON

OK. Let me put Lilly's tape on.

ARLEN

Really?

WILSON

Look is it my birthday or isn't it?

LILLY (V.O. IN BACKGROUND)

In the province of the mind, what one believes to be true, either is true or becomes true within certain limits. These limits are to be found experimentally and experientially. When so found these limits turn out to be further beliefs to be transcended. In the province of the mind there are no limits.

ARLEN

Why this?

WILSON

It encourages gullibility. No scepticism allowed while the experiment is on. It just prevents interesting results.

ARLEN

Oh, so this is an experiment now?

WILSON

An erotic experiment.

They kiss deeply.

WILSON

The Crowley invocation is on here too. Is that OK with you?

ARLEN

So long as I get my gift of tongues you can play any weird shit you like, lover boy.

WILSON

I'm just gonna get the sage.

Arlen slumps in frustration. Wilson lights candles and fans sage towards the four directions.

WILSON

You sit here. This is your throne. Every man a priest, every woman a priestess, every home a shrine.

> He undresses her slowly, and very lovingly.

ARLEN

"Children of a future age, Reading this indignant page, Know that in a former time, Love, sweet love, was thought a crime."

WILSON

Blake. "I think I see God when I look upon my lady nude".

ARLEN

Vidal. Does this make us members of the Illuminati?

WILSON

From what I can gather, this is just the beginning of a long journey . They say there's just as much discipline needed to practice Tantra as Hatha yoga, and as much capacity for loving and giving of oneself as Bhakti yoga.

ARLEN
(as she lies back)

It's a difficult path, but somebody's got to walk it.

WILSON

OK. Gift of tongues comes later. First you need to learn the breath.

ARLEN

Breath?

WILSON

The breath is very important. In like you're sucking through a straw. It's a breath which feeds the body instead of the mind.

> Arlen begins to do the breath. They find their rhythm. They breathe together for some time.

ARLEN

The walls, Bob! The walls are breathing.

> The walls are indeed breathing.

WILSON

OK. Now you visualise the Kundalini energy rising up through the centre of your body. The breath helps you to suck the energy all the way through your body.

ARLEN

What happens when it gets to the top?

WILSON

You circle it back round to the root chakra. OK. Crowley's invocation is coming in now.

> Unseen, the full cast, in black ceremonial robes have gathered circling Arlen and Wilson and the audience. They hold candles and begin to incant.

CAST

Spirit most holy! Seed most Wise!
Innocent Babe, Inviolate Maid!
Begetter of Being! Soul of all Souls!
Word of all Words,
Come forth, most hidden Light.
Devour thou me! Thou dost devour Me!

> Arlen and Wilson's rhythmic breathing is amplified and the murmur of Lilly's "Beliefs Unlimited" continues beneath the incantation.

CAST

Spirit most holy! Seed most Wise!
Innocent Babe, Inviolate Maid!
Begetter of Being! Soul of all Souls!
Word of all Words,
Come forth, most hidden Light.
Devour thou me! Thou dost devour Me!

> Arlen is now astride Wilson, both sat upright (yab-yum position). The sound of breathing, the changing colours, Lilly's voice, the Crowley incantation and the music lifts the energy still further . . .

The hooded figures envelop the bed, masking it momentarily. They part and disperse, revealing Wilson now locked in ecstasy with a Silver Space Lady.

> The breathing, the incantation, the colours and the moaning build and build–

EVERYONE
(as if suddenly possessed)

It is time for life on Earth to leave the planetary womb. The goal of evolution is to produce nervous systems capable of communicating with and returning to the Galactic Network where we, your interstellar parents await you. We love you! We yearn for you. Put on the wings, and arouse the coiled splendor within you: come unto me! The time has come for you to accept the responsibility of immortality. It is not necessary for you to die. Mutate! Come home in glory.

> The effects stop. The Space lady is gone. Seemingly impossibly, Arlen appears behind the audience.

WILSON

Who am I?

ARLEN

Husband, and father and mystic and friend.

WILSON

Skeptic.

ARLEN

And shaman. And investigator.

WILSON

That psychic said I was a Chinese Sage in another life. Or a member of the Illuminati.

ARLEN

You are Bob.

WILSON

Am I though? You ask me. Who are you?

ARLEN

Who are you?

WILSON

A domesticated primate.

ARLEN

Who are you?

WILSON

Consciousness apprehending . . .

ARLEN

Who are you?

WILSON

A man.

ARLEN

Who are you?

WILSON

An event.

ARLEN

Who are you?

WILSON

Love.

ARLEN

Who are you?

WILSON

A speck on a rock floating round a star.

ARLEN

Who are you?

WILSON
(stage whisper)

I think I might have been spiked.

ARLEN

What?

WILSON
(In actor's own voice)

OK – this isn't funny.

ARLEN
(trying to get back to the script)

Who are you?

WILSON
(in actor's own voice)

I haven't got the faintest idea. OK – whoever has done this – it isn't funny.

ARLEN

Who are you?

ACTOR (Wilson)

Some acid head from the 70s?

ARLEN

Who are you?

ACTOR

A science fiction author?

ARLEN

Who are you?

ACTOR

Ok, Bollocks to this – Ken?

KEN
(from audience)

What's up?

ACTOR

I think someone has spiked me backstage before this rehearsal.

KEN

Yeah, quite possibly, but this isn't a rehearsal.

ARLEN

Who are you?

ACTOR

I think you need to stop this play.

KEN

Yeah, problem is , I'm just an actor too.

ARLEN

Who are you?

ACTOR

Jesus, stop asking that.

ARLEN

It's the next line of the script. Who are you?

ACTOR

Do you know what? Sod this.

> He begins to exit.

DAISY
(from audience)

It's OK. Your name is Oliver Senton.

> *NB: The actor playing Wilson's real name.*

You're an actor in a play. You're playing Robert Anton Wilson – and you're doing a fantastic job. These are all the people who've come to see you.

ACTOR

Who are you?

DAISY

I'm Daisy, I've written the play, based on a book and another play which was based on another book.

ACTOR

You're not Daisy.

DAISY

Yes I am.

ACTOR

No you're not

REAL DAISY

No, alright, I am – she's the heroic stage-manager playing me. Can we please get back to the show?

ACTOR

Why?

DAISY

Why are we doing this show?

ACTOR

Yes.

DAISY

Because in the words of Timothy Leary, once you've turned on, tuned in and dropped out, the next thing you gotta do is find the others. Is that right?

REAL DAISY

Something like that.

ACTOR

What others are we finding?

DAISY

The others who have also realised that it's all a play.

(weighty pause)

Is that right?

REAL DAISY

Yeah, it sounds a bit tossy now I hear it out loud.

ACTOR

And there's another reality beyond this one?

REAL DAISY

I guess.

ACTOR

And beyond that one?

Real Daisy shrugs.

KEN ACTOR

We are deep in the heart of Chapel Perilous now seekers.

ACTOR

Is this the illumination of the Illuminati – to experience scepticism to the point where it abolishes itself and, since you can't believe anything fully, you are as free of scepticism as any other philosophy and finally open to thinking the unthinkable?

REAL DAISY

Sounds good. Shall we get back to the scene? Arlen can we take it from Who are You?

ARLEN

Who are you?

ACTOR

Oliver Senton?

> Arlen looks at Real Daisy, unsure.
>
> Real Daisy indicates for her to keep going.

ARLEN

Who are you?

ACTOR

An ancient Chinese Sage?

ARLEN

Who are you?

ACTOR

Secret head of the Illuminati?

ARLEN

Who are you?

ACTOR

Robert Anton Wilson.

ARLEN
(resuming the lovemaking)

Who are you?

WILSON

Robert Anton Wilson, besotted husband of Arlen Wilson, with whom right at this very moment I am making love.

ARLEN
(more ecstatic)

Who are you?

WILSON

An enormous heart, exploding with love for you.

ARLEN

Who – are – you?

WILSON

Energy

ARLEN

Who – are – you?

WILSON

Consciousness

ARLEN
(pure ecstasy)

Who are we?

WILSON

Union. Perfect – union.

Black out.

2.7: THE MORNING AFTER

> Wilson and Arlen are both blissfully asleep. Wilson wakes up suddenly with a jolt. He scrambles around for a notebook and pen.

> FUCKUP (V.O.)
> (A booming voice)

July 23rd 1973: Sirius is very important.

> Wilson leaps up and rifles through his piles of books. Arlen wakes up as if to heaven itself.

> ARLEN

My God. That was the most extraordinary . . . experiment . . . of my life. It was like – Oh I can't even begin to explain it.

> WILSON

Sirius is very important.

> ARLEN

What?

WILSON

I woke up with a powerful message: Sirius is very important. There was more to it, but that's all I can remember.

ARLEN

What are you looking for?

WILSON

The Magical Revival book. It might have a reference to Sirius.

> He lets the book fall open.

(reading)

Crowley identified the heart of his magical current with one particular star. In occult tradition this is the sun behind the sun, the hidden God, the vast star Sirius.

ARLEN

Jesus.

WILSON

I think I need to go to the library.

> He exits.

ARLEN

Oh, OK. I was kind of hoping for a re-run of the Holy Gift of Tongues –

> The front door slams.

ARLEN

Guess not.

2.8: MOON INTERLUDE

> Simon Moon and a beautiful
> woman are in a jacuzzi

MOON

You never really looked at a dollar bill before, now did you? The symbol of the pyramid is alchemical of course. The traditional code represents the three kinds of sex by a pyramid, a sphere and a cube. The travesty that we call normal sex is represented by the cube in which the two nervous systems never actually merge at the orgasm; like the parallel sides of the cube. The pyramid has the two sides coming together; the magical telepathic orgasm. The sphere is that Tantric ritual, endlessly prolonged, with no orgasm at all. The alchemists used that code for over two thousand years. The Rosicrucians used the symbol of the pyramid for their kind of weird sex magic. Aleister Crowley used the same symbol quite recently.

KEN
(stood in audience)

Yeah, it's quite good. As long as we've got enough bubbles. Right. Shall we call it a night. Where's everyone else gone?

MOON ACTOR

It's past 3am, Ken.

KEN

Oh well we could do another couple of hours then.

2.9: SIRIUS CONTACT

> Arlen is setting the table, as Wilson arrives looking discombobulated.

ARLEN

Dinner will be ready in ten. Kids are back. So much for our romantic weekend. Find anything interesting at the library?

WILSON

I discovered that this very day, July 23rd, is the day, according to Egyptian tradition, when the occult link is most powerful between Earth and Sirius.

ARLEN

Mm hmm?

WILSON

Yes. And there's a voice.

ARLEN

A voice?

WILSON

Yeah, it's been with me all day. It's told me which books to look into – which page to turn to. A kind of – angelic voice. And it claims to be from Sirius.

ARLEN

Is that a . . . good thing?

WILSON

I don't know, Arlen. Also, I keep getting these really clear flashes of Tim. He's doing all these experiments with telepathy, trying to fly over the prison walls.

ARLEN

Well maybe you should talk to him about it.

WILSON

I can't. Nothing is getting through now he's in maximum security. Arlen, I'm a bit freaked. The voice and the visions are so real. Oh, God, am I completely destroying my mind?

> Wilson doesn't notice Arlen leaving, and a Sirius Alien entering.

WILSON
(to audience)

Or, had I actually – through Crowley's invocation – turned on and tuned in to an Earth-Sirius channel used by adepts since ancient Egypt?

SIRIAN ALIEN

Post's here my love.

> Wilson absent-mindedly takes the post, without realising his wife is now an alien from Sirius.

WILSON
(To audience)

In October I finally received permission to correspond with Tim. In my first letter I very carefully did not mention my July 23rd experience with Sirius or my visions of Tim himself. I was still fairly sure my impression that Tim was doing telepathic experiments in July was accurate, but I didn't want to say anything just yet.

LEARY

Dear Bob. Loved your letter. The prison administration is perfect. They act as a Van Allen belt protecting my privacy, screening out distraction. The Warden is like a gruff Zen abbot. He doesn't want me to be bothered with visits or correspondence that would bring me down, slow up my scientific work etc.

WILSON

The next part of his reply blew my mind.

LEARY

I need to know something: are you in touch with teachings, methods, teachers, etc that transmit Higher Intelligence? In July I formed a four-person telepathy team here at the prison in an attempt to contact Higher Intelligences elsewhere in the galaxy. The result of our experiments I have named The Starseed Experiment.

WILSON
(to audience)

So Leary had received these transmissions in the middle of the Dog Days when I was having my first (real or hallucinatory) contacts with Sirius, and also the recurring vision that Leary was engaging in some kind of telepathy.

Curiouser and curiouser.

SIRIAN ALIEN

Leary is also contacting us. Contact Joanna Leary for a copy of Terra II.

WILSON

I contacted Joanna for a copy of Terra II.

SIRIAN ALIEN

Open the door, there's a package arriving.

> The doorbell rings.

DELIVERY MAN

Mr Wilson? You ordered a copy of The Sirius Mysteries by Robert K.G. Temple? There you go, sign there. It's a rather far-fetched theory. According to him an advanced race from another planet visited Earth around 4500BC. But he is a Fellow of the Royal Astronomical Society of England, and his evidence is very compelling.

WILSON
(astonished)

Wha – well, I . . .

SIRIAN ALIEN

Say thank you.

WILSON

Thank you.

> Delivery man exits.

NB: In a couple of London performances the delivery man was accompanied by Robert Temple himself, who introduced himself to Bob (they failed to meet in Bob's lifetime). This was our glorious Annie-Hall-style Marshall McLuhan moment.

WILSON
(to audience)

Reading Temple's book was like opening a door in my own house and finding Ming the Merciless shooting it out with Flash Gordon.

SIRIAN ALIEN

Now strive to be the best father and husband you can be.

WILSON

And then I did my best to become a father and a husband again.

2.10: LUNA PAINTS THE WHITE LIGHT

Lights up on Luna (now approximately 12) painting on an easel, as she sings a lilting tune.

WILSON
(to Luna)

What are you painting darling?

LUNA

I'm trying to paint the clear light.

WILSON

It's beautiful.

> He watches her paint for a while.

How's your face?

> Luna turns around, revealing a swollen black eye. Wilson flinches.

Those damned boys. Karma really is a blind machine.

LUNA

No dad. I've stopped the wheel of karma. All the bad feeling is with the boys who beat me up. Not with me.

> Wilson pours her some juice.

WILSON

I think you understand more about life than I ever will. There you go, darling. Foot Doot.

> They settle down together at the kitchen table.

LUNA

Is the Sirius woman still talking to you?

                              WILSON

Yes, all the time. Don't mention it to your mother.

                               LUNA

What does she say?

                              WILSON

Silly things.

                               LUNA

Like what?

                              WILSON

She tells me that I will be much happier if I forgive.

                               LUNA

That's true.

                              WILSON

I guess I thought I was too sophisticated to need messages like that, but I've taken her advice. I've forgiven my publisher for being a schmuck and I do feel happier. I guess I should have figured that out when I was your age – but somehow I never did.

                               LUNA

What else?

                              WILSON

She's very concerned that I should look into time more.

                               LUNA

Time?

WILSON

That I should try to understand the nature of time. It seems to be very important.

LUNA

And have you?

WILSON

Not really.

LUNA

Dad.

WILSON

Everything she says about Time is completely incomprehensible. But I've done a bit of research, and it seems that everything scientists say about time is equally incomprehensible. I did a ritual about it, but it didn't throw much up.

LUNA

Do you believe she's really from Sirius?

WILSON

The truth is sweetheart, I got a bit scared. Because everything seemed to point towards it being for real. Yeah, I started to believe it. So I decided to convince myself that it was just my right brain talking to my left brain. And the world provided a great deal of evidence for that too. The voices and the synchronicity completely stopped.

LUNA

But you liked having her around . . . ?

WILSON

I had a good long talk with myself, and decided that this whole Sirius thing may be an important part of whatever this quest is that I'm on. So I've decided for the sake of my meta-programming experiments to adopt the belief system that I am in contact with an extraterrestrial. Don't tell your mother.

LUNA

In a way it's like trying on different costumes to get a feel for different types of people.

>Wilson smiles at this thought.

So – tell me more stuff she tells you.

WILSON

She quite often tells me silly things about people. Like their star sign.

LUNA

Their star sign?!

WILSON

Just turns me into a darn carnival act.

LUNA

I think it's cool.

WILSON

I seem to know when there'll be a knock at the door or when the phone's going to ring and half the time who'll be on the other end.

>There's a knock at the door.

LUNA
(laughing)

Well, who's there?

WILSON

I've absolutely no idea. But I'll bet they're a Gemini!

> Luna exits. Wilson answers the door. Kerry is outside, looking worse for wear.

Kerry! Wow, how you doing man? It's been a long time.

KERRY

Yeah, yeah. Can I come in? I don't want to be seen.

WILSON
(confused)

Yeah, sure.

> They go in.

A beer, some coffee, some sweet Mary Jane?

KERRY

Yeah, yeah.

> Kerry stalks about, looking for clues.

WILSON

So?

KERRY

So? So you say? You don't have the slightest fucking clue what's been going on do you? You spoken to Greg?

WILSON

I've been out of the loop, Kerry. Working on this Illuminatus thing.

KERRY

Yeah, Bob, you pedal your made-up conspiracy bullshit all you like. I'm living it.

WILSON

What's going on Kerry? Sit down. Fill me in.

> Kerry keeps pacing. He talks fast.

KERRY

At the moment I have every reason to believe I'm going down for 20 years in a Louisiana prison.

WILSON

Jesus. What for?

KERRY

What for? What the fuck for? Jesus Bob where you been? Up your own asshole? For my part in the conspiracy to kill President John F Kennedy.

WILSON

Waa?

KERRY

OK. Shit. So you know I was in the marines with Lee Harvey Oswald, right? So when I was there I heard him talking to this Russian dude. So Jim Garrison –

WILSON

The lawyer who's investigating the assassination?

KERRY

Yeah, man. You been living in a box? Garrison's whole line of enquiry collapsed, but he's determined to nail someone at least for perjury, so he can keep his whole circus running. So who's testimony does he choose to move on to? Only fucking yours truly. So now I'm subpoenaed to appear before a New Orleans grand jury. It's a fucking mad hatter's tea party. But listen, on the way to the courthouse I bump into this old pal Slim Brooks. He asks if I'm planning to mention anything to Garrison about Brother-in-law.

WILSON

Brother-in-law?

KERRY

This guy I knew when I was like 19. Gary Kirstein was his real name. You remember Olga? The writer from the French quarter? I introduced you at that acid party?

WILSON

Oh yeah. Beautiful.

KERRY

Yeah, not any more. She shot herself in the head.

WILSON

Fuck.

KERRY

Yeah, so she was knocking about with this Gary guy. Then out of the blue she fucking kills herself, right? So anyway to Slim I'm thinking – what's this got to do with this Gary guy – this fucking Brother-in-law? Am I going to mention my conversations with Gary? No, as it turns out I'm not into stirring up Garrison's paranoia about me any further by bringing up each and every time I had bullshitted about assassinating JFK with someone. Anyway Garrison fired a load of names at me in court that day, but Gary Kirstein was not one of them.

WILSON

But you think he's significant?

KERRY

Listen, man. He had me working for him back then. Research stuff. He sent me to the library for this book about Nazism he was supposedly writing and I had to copy out in notebooks all the weirdest, most depraved Nazi shit I could find. And then I would have to put my name to it. Where are those notebooks? Fucking Garrison has got them. And then another thing, whenever Gary got a chance he'd introduce me as "a friend of Oswald's. A whole fucking number of witnesses remember it. And they remember me saying, "oh yeah, I masterminded the whole assassination".

WILSON

And you wrote a book about Oswald didn't you?

KERRY

And I wrote that fucking book. Before the fucking assassination. Before anyone had even heard of Lee Fucking Harvey Fucking Oswald.

WILSON

Fuck, man.

KERRY

I'm up to my ass in a cheap spy novel. I am the victim of either the most fantastic chain of incriminating coincidences or the most satanically evil plot in history.

WILSON

Have you spoken to anyone about– how you're feeling about all this?

KERRY

Like who?

WILSON

Well, like a doctor, I guess.

KERRY

Oh yeah, yeah. Of course they said I was clinically paranoid. But I said to them, "How can you make that diagnosis when you haven't even read the Warren Commission report?"

WILSON
(taking it in)

Eris is fucking you sideways, backwards and upside down.

KERRY

Did you know that the first five copies of *Principia Discordia* were run off on Jim Garrison's xerox machine? Greg was screwing his secretary back then.

WILSON

You're shitting me? So Eris herself was birthed in Garrison's office?

KERRY

I tell you something, man. If I'd have known it was all going to come true, I'd never have chosen that bitch Eris. I'd have chosen Venus.

>Luna enters quietly.

LUNA

Hi Kerry.

KERRY

Oh, hi Kid.

LUNA

Kerry, are you a Gemini?

KERRY
(leaping up, utterly paranoid)

Yeah, how the hell do you know that?

2.11: LIVERPOOL PERFORMANCE 1976

The audience can now see both the stage of the Liverpool production of *Illuminatus!*, and backstage.

NB: In fact Illuminatus! was staged in Liverpool on multiple miniature stages (built by Bill Drummond of The KLF) wrapping around the audience.

MAVIS

First of all, most of what you've been told here is bullshit. The Illuminati have no 14 millennia old history. They invented their great heritage and tradition out of cloth in 1776. We've done the same. You might be wondering, "Why do we copy them and even deceive our own recruits about this?" Well, part of Illumination is learning to doubt everything. That's why Hassan I Sabbah said, "Nothing is true, everything is permitted," and why Hagbard has that painting that says "Think for yourself, Schmuck". There are no honest men on this voyage. In fact, maybe this part is the only lie I've told you all evening, and the Illuminati history really is true and not an invention. Or maybe we're just a front for the Illuminati. Feeling paranoid? Good. Illumination is on the other side of absolute terror, and the only terror that is absolute is the horror of realising that you can't believe anything you've ever been told and you cannot even trust your own mind.

> Mavis exits from the stage to backstage. She's now Prunella Gee, or Prue.

KEN

Prue, fucking brilliant. Brought the house down.

PRUE

Thanks Ken.

KEN

Has anyone seen Bill Drummond? One of the sets is falling apart.

PRUE

Yes, he's gone off to get some glue for it. He had a funny look in his eye. Muttering something about Mu Mu?

> Chris (playing George Dorn) walks past.

KEN

Chris stand further away from that new bloke in the next submarine bit.

CHRIS

Oh alright. How far back?

KEN

He's totally fucking inaudible. Stand behind the audience and we might be in with a chance.

PRUE

Is Peter Hall enjoying it?

KEN

He's having the Bard blown right out of the back of his head. It's the greatest show on Planet World!

(to passing actor)

Listen, the black mass scene? When you put the girl on the altar I want you stark naked and covered in goat's blood.

ACTOR

Stark naked?

KEN

Yeah.

ACTOR

Oh, OK. Where do I find the goat's blood?

KEN

Christ, I don't know everything.

Actor scurries off

PRUE

Ken. This is magical. No-one here will ever forget this.

As Miss Portinari goes onstage, Ken pulls Prue towards him.

KEN

Come on, this is quite a long speech.

They kiss. They move into darkness and the stage becomes lit.

A bird's eye view of the tarot scene, in one of Bill Drummond's infamous sets.

MISS PORTINARI

It's the story of the development of the soul. We call it a book – the *Book of Thoth* – and it's the most important book in the world. But the order was deliberately reversed. Here let me show you. The last card, Trump 21, is really the first. It's where we all start from. This is the Abyss of Hallucinations. This is where our attention is usually focused. It is entirely constructed by our senses and our projected emotions, as modern psychology and ancient Buddhism both testify – but it is what most people call "reality." They are conditioned to accept it, and not to inquire further, because only in this dream-walking state can they be governed by those who wish to govern.

> As this speech goes on, Ken and Prue return to the spotlight.

PRUE

Ken, listen. There's something I've been meaning to tell you. I'm pregnant.

ACTOR
(Naked and covered in goats blood)

Does this look convincing enough?

KEN
(looking at the Actor)

Pregnant?

ACTOR
(confused)

No. Stark naked and covered in goat's blood.

> On stage.

MISS PORTINARI
(with force)

Only in this dream-walking state can they be governed by those who wish to govern.

> Backstage.

PRUE

Shit. I'm on.

> And she's in the bright stage lights.
>
> *NB: Prunella Gee is Daisy Campbell's mother.*

PRUE (AS MAVIS)

Do you begin to see the full dimensions of our struggle with the Illuminati? You Sir, do you see the full dimensions? No? All right, well at least for now you can probably grasp this much: their fundamental fallacy is the aneristic delusion.

HAGBARD

An-eristic.

MAVIS

Look at the Pentagon – look at the whole army for Goddess's sake! That's what they want the planet to be like. Efficient, mechanical, orderly – and inhuman. That's the essence of the aneristic delusion – to imagine you have found order and then to start manipulating the quirky, eccentric, chaotic things that really exist into some kind of platoons or phalanxes that correspond to your concept of the order they're supposed to manifest. Of course, the quirkiest, most chaotic things that exist are other people – and that's why they're so obsessed with trying to control us.

> As she speaks, the clacking of a typewriter can be heard over her words, then Wilson's voice joins the speech, then Mavis is mouthing the words, and we hear just Wilson. The lights fade on Mavis and come up on Wilson and Shea.

2.12: FINISHING ILLUMINATUS!

WILSON

Ok let's go back to that bit – It was the sound of the eternal and unending clash between I and AM and their unity in I AM, he even thought for a flash of the critics of hunting and how little they understood of this secret, this mystic identity between the killer and the killed –

> Shea types furiously to keep up with the flow of ideas.

SHEA

– but he had it, it was in the sight, he breathed, he aimed, he slacked, he squeezed, death in life and life in death. It was falling, plunging downward, the most heart breaking beautiful sight he had ever seen –

WILSON

– it would last as long as human speech survived, and he had done it, he had achieved immortality, he had taken its life and now it was part of him. His nose was running and his eyes were watering. "I did it," he screamed to the mountains, "I did it! I killed the last American eagle!"

SHEA

The earth below him cracked.

> Shea and Wilson look at each other and slowly realise they have got to the end.

SHEA

We did it. We wrote The Great Discordian Epic American Novel.

> They hug each other for a long time. Shea exits.

WILSON
(dreamily)

I can't believe we did it. I!

> Remembering, he bites himself hard on the thumb.

(to audience)

Oh you can laugh, but you try it. Go on – go and have a break – and here's your challenge:

Do not utter that myth of a word

(he mouths the word 'I')

for the entire interval. 23 minutes. And I expect you to bite your thumbs if you do . . .

Oh shit.

> He exits, biting his thumb.

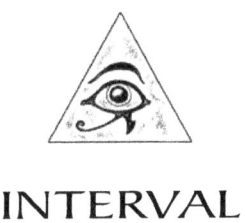

INTERVAL

ACT THREE

3.1: ERIS RETURNS

WILSON

So – sore thumbs, ladies and gentlemen? But just a little closer to realising what a convenient fiction that innocuous little word is?

We finished *Illuminatus*, but if we'd known it would be a further five years of grinding poverty and hell before there was even a whiff of it getting published, perhaps we'd have saved the celebrations. With that Magnum Opus out of the way, my Mystic turned his attention back to the Sirius mystery.

ERIS
(uncharacteristically sweet and gentle)

Before you do all that boring stuff I want to show everyone my new apple.

WILSON

Eris, my Goddess, could we just keep our strange tale on track for a bit without your interruptions?

ERIS

Of course you bloody can't. I'm the Goddess of Choas and Confusion not the Goddess of Keeping your Strange Tale on Track. And – must I once again remind you – you chose me! Anyway this lot want to see what I've got in my Golden Apple don't you? Or should I say who? A real troublemaker in here – one of my most trusted chaos creators. You all want to see, don't you?

> After whipping up the audience, she lifts the lid of the golden apple to reveal a different chaos merchant each night.

Chaos ensues for 3 minutes.

NB: Over the course of our 23 London 2017 performances we encountered: anarchic dancers, pyromaniacs, obscene burlesque, crooning Cthulhu and money burning amongst much else . . .

WILSON

May I now return to the Sirius evidence?

ERIS

Oh yes, return to your Sirius evidence. You fruitcake.

WILSON

Let us review some of our evidence. I became obsessed with the number 23 and the eye-in-the-triangle design years before I found any link between them and Sirius. After July 23rd I definitely experienced impressions which I thought were communications from Sirius, keyed off by a Crowley ritual. Kenneth Grant, one of Crowley's closest associates repeatedly links Crowley with Sirius and seems to hint that the Holy Guardian Angel contacted by Crowleyan mind-expansion techniques is a denizen of Sirius. J.G Bennett, close ally of Gurdjieff tells us of coded references to Sirius in Gurdjieff's writings. George Hunt Williamson, a flying saucer contactee, claims to have spoken to natives of Sirius who use a language containing some of the same words as the Enochian language used by John Dee. Williamson also claims that a secret order on Earth has been in contact with Sirius for thousands of years and that the emblem of that order is the eye of Horus or the eye-in-the-pyramid. And finally we have Temple's evidence, in a book that emerged at the same time that myself and Leary were apparently making some kind of extraterrestrial contact, based on the Dogon tribe of Africa which had advanced knowledge of the Sirius system long before scientists discovered it with their telescopes. This, I feel, represents at minimum an extraordinary amount of coincidence . . .

ARLEN

Are you still writing?

WILSON

I know, I'll stop.

ARLEN

Are you coming to bed?

WILSON

I just want to do my evening meditation.

ARLEN

I'll join you.

> The two of them sit down to meditate side by side. Some time passes. A severe jolt runs through Wilson.

ARLEN

What's happened, Bob?

WILSON

It's nothing.

ARLEN

Tell me.

WILSON

I just had a premonition about Graham.

ARLEN

What?

WILSON

It's probably nothing.

ARLEN

Tell me the truth, Bob.

WILSON

I heard a voice tell me that Graham will –

ARLEN

Will what, Bob?

WILSON

Die soon. It's nothing. Parental paranoia.

ARLEN

Was it with that same feeling you talk about? Bob?

WILSON
(very reluctantly)

I was in that ESP alpha state.

ARLEN

Shit, Bob. I wish you'd never got us mixed up with this Crowleyan shit.

Arlen exits

WILSON

I'll do some protective rites. It's probably all bullshit. Arlen?

She's gone.

Hear my prayers, if I have seen into the future, hear my prayers to deflect this from happening. Do not let this happen! Or if you cannot deflect it, give me the strength to bear it.

Pause.

Wilson shakes it off, convincing himself the premonition was nonsense.

WILSON
(to audience)

Then acceptance of my request to visit Tim Leary in jail came through, and I realised I was deep in the heart of Chapel Perilous. All my maps had well and truly run out.

3.2: A VISIT TO LEARY IN PRISON

At California Medical Facility or CMF, the prison where Leary now resides.

Leary is led out to the table where Wilson is waiting. He has the big Leary grin on his face. The Prison Guard unlocks his handcuffs, scowling.

LEARY

Bob!

Leary looks into Wilson's eyes, with the inoffensive curiosity of an infant.

You are in great shape!

WILSON

You look great too. How are you doing? I heard this prison has a reputation that Dr. Frankenstein's laboratory can hardly beat.

LEARY

Well, yes. The methods of psycho-surgery and aversive therapy they use to cure sexual deviates have more in common with Bull Conners' cattle-prods than with anything therapeutic; but that's the psychiatric side of Vacaville, where they keep people they think they're trying to help. On this side, it's purely punitive, so it's much more humane.

WILSON

Well, I'm glad you ended up on this side.

LEARY

It was never in doubt, Bob. I wrote the Psych tests they use!

> They sit themselves down at the table. Around them, other inmates talk to their visitors.

Your last letter amazed me, Bob. You must begin corresponding at once with an English poet named Brian Barritt. You cannot write another line until you have gotten your heads in synch. You are both exploring the same elephant from two sides.

WILSON

I have a few elephants on the go?

LEARY

Crowley.

WILSON

Ah, that elephant.

LEARY

When I was in exile in Switzerland I was shown a deck of Crowley's Tarot cards. So to test their divinatory power I asked, "who am I and what is my destiny?" I got the Ace of Disks.

WILSON

TO MEGA THERION. The Great Beast. Crowley's name for himself.

LEARY

Which of course I interpret to mean that I am Crowley reborn and I'm supposed to complete the work which Crowley began, preparing humanity for cosmic consciousness.

>He lets out a loud, raucous laugh.

WILSON

Of course.

LEARY

Confessions of a Hope Fiend. Name of my next book.

WILSON

I like it.

LEARY

Did you read about my work on higher neurological circuits turned on by psychedelics?

WILSON

Just what you mentioned in your letter.

LEARY

And you've heard about the telepathic work I'm doing with a group of four other inmates? Starseed?

WILSON

Yes, in fact I think you began to receive those transmissions at the same time I made my Sirian contact.

LEARY

Really? Good God, the plot thickens. Yes, it's my emerging belief that these higher circuits evolved for use in outer space, not merely for getting blissed out on our Earth side trip.

WILSON

So you think we have eight circuits?

> All the other inmates' and visitors' faces snap to face front, then immediately go back to their conversations. Wilson and Leary don't see it, but the effect is momentarily disconcerting.

LEARY

Potentially, yes. All the shamans and mystics who opened the four higher circuits knew they had something to do with cosmic energy, but they didn't know the why, the how, the next step.

WILSON

And the lower four?

LEARY

The first four are linear and designed for use on Earth. Circuit One: Bio-survival or Physical intelligence.

> MUSIC: The Eight Circuit song. This one should rock the joint. Leary and Wilson stand on tables holding microphones, and the Prisoners and Visitors dance and sing around them, in perfectly synched choreography.

PRISONERS AND VISITORS
(whispering rhythmically)

Tit! Bark! Maps! Sex! Turn on, Get Cosmic!
Tit! Bark! Maps! Sex! Turn on, Get Cosmic!
Tit! Bark! Maps! Sex! Turn on, Get Cosmic!

ENSEMBLE
(singing)

Eight Circuits, eight circuits – don't blow a fuse
Robotic behaviour – is scripted to lose
Come be a winner, a meta-programmer
Don't panic, don't panic
You're a karma mechanic

PRISONERS AND VISITORS
(spoken over the riff)

Tit! Bark! Maps! Sex! Turn on, Get Cosmic!

PRISONER 1
(spoken, to audience)

I don't know how I ended up in here. I guess my mother left when I was still a babe in arms – Maybe that smack made me feel like I was back in her lovin' arms. Or should I say – back suckling that almighty tit.

LEARY
(singing)

Bio-survival! It's totallly primal!
What is the imprint that makes you a mammal?
Cosy and cuddly and suckling your mummy
This first circuit is ancient and deep

WILSON
(speaks soulfully into the mic)

A good imprint and you've got a basic attitude of trust. Get it wrong, and it will lead to a basic attitude of suspicion.

ENSEMBLE

Eight Circuits, eight circuits – don't blow a fuse
Robotic behaviour is scripted to lose

Come be a winner, a meta-programmer
Don't panic, don't panic
You're a Karma Mechanic
Tit! Bark! Maps! Sex! Turn on, Get Cosmic!

PRISONER 2

Hey! You looking at my girl?

PRISONER 3

Why'd I wanna look at that dog?

> The prisoners and visitors get into a huge fight and all fall to the ground barking like dogs.

LEARY
(singing)

Emotional and territorial
We must have moved to circuit two,
Ego and Status make us fighters and haters
The world is run on circuit two

WILSON

Like you always say, The only intelligent way to discuss politics is –

LEARY & WILSON

On all fours!

ENSEMBLE

Eight Circuits, eight circuits – don't blow a fuse
Robotic behaviour is scripted to lose
Come be a winner, a meta-programmer
Don't panic, don't panic

You're a Karma Mechanic
Tit! Bark! Maps! Sex! Turn on, Get Cosmic!

VISITOR 1

So I applied to that geography course you told me I shouldn't bother with, Frank.

PRISONER 3

Why do you want to go and humiliate yourself like that?

VISITOR 1

And I got on it, Frank. Unlike you I'm gonna make something of myself.

PRISONER 3

Hey you wanna spend your life looking at maps that's your funeral.

LEARY
(singing)

Circuit three: the Symbolic
Concepts and tools and theories and rules
Sensation and feeling gives way to reason
This is Map-building logic

WILSON

Learning more about everything, including how to learn!

ENSEMBLE

Eight Circuits, eight circuits – don't blow a fuse
Robotic behaviour is scripted to lose –

> A Prison Guard appears. The number stops dead, and the scene returns to normal. He walks slowly

and suspiciously through the tables. The party begins again as soon as he's out of sight.

Come be a winner, a meta-programmer
Don't panic, don't panic
You're a Karma Mechanic

Tit! Bark! Maps! Sex! Turn on, Get Cosmic!

PRISONER 2

So I'm getting it on in the privacy of my own car. Got my dick in this fine little mouth. All is sweet. Then my pa he has to shine his goddamn torch in the car. His face when he saw I was getting sucked off by a boy. Well, you can see I had no choice. I had to kill 'em both. And I ain't got it up since.

LEARY
(singing)

Drop to the floor for circuit four
What turns you off and on
Socio-sexual the drive is perpetual
To get your freak on
But if you have a kink that you cannot mention
Say hello, my friend, to a life of repression

ENSEMBLE

Life of repression, life of repression. Life of repression, life of repression

WILSON
(spoken)

It seems as we make our way through these circuits up to adolescence we pay a heavy price.

LEARY

Oh yeah, Bob. The ultimate sacrifice. Our survival and status means forfeiting the infinite possibilities of unconditioned consciousness.

Those first four circuits narrow the polymorphous infant into an adjusted adult with one personality, one sex-role, one system of co-ordinates – usually conservative and mildly paranoid, to mesh with the conservative and mildly paranoid local value system. The other four, still-evolving circuits have traditionally been activated by shamans and mystics and now through psychedelic experience.

WILSON

What are they?

Total change in musical vibe.

LEARY
(singing)

They're neuro-somatic, neuro-electric, neuro-genetic and psycho-atomic

ENSEMBLE

Neuro-somatic, neuro-electric, neuro-genetic and psycho-atomic. Turn on, tune in, mutate, go cosmic!

LEARY

Or one could say; Sensory, Psychic, Mythic and Spiritual

PRISONER 1

Sensory

WILSON

Loser:

PRISONER 1

I can't help the way I feel.

LEARY

Winner:

PRISONER 2

How I feel depends on my neurological know-how.

ENSEMBLE

Neuro-somatic, neuro-electric, neuro-genetic and psycho-atomic. Turn on, tune in, mutate – go cosmic!

WILSON

Psychic

LEARY

Loser?

PRISONER 3

Why do I have such lousy luck?

WILSON

Winner?

PRISONER 4

I make my own coincidences, synchronicities, luck and destiny.

ENSEMBLE

Neuro-somatic, neuro-electric, neuro-genetic and psycho-atomic. Turn on, tune in, mutate – go cosmic!

WILSON

Mythic

LEARY

Loser?

PRISONER 5

Evolution is blind and impersonal.

WILSON

Winner?

PRISONER 6

Future evolution depends on my decisions now.

ENSEMBLE

Neuro-somatic, neuro-electric, neuro-genetic and psycho-atomic. Turn on, tune in, mutate – go cosmic!

WILSON

Loser:

PRISONER 7
(in handcuffs)

I'm not psychic and I doubt that anyone is.

EVERYONE

Winner:

PRISONER 7
(breaks open handcuffs)

Nothing is true, everything is permitted!

EVERYONE

Starseed! Starseed! Starseed! Starseed! Starseeeeeeed!

The back of the prison wall falls away, revealing we are all inside a spaceship hurtling towards the stars.

3.3: CROWLEYMAS

> The Wilsons' home. Luna is heading out the door. Wilson is sitting at his typewriter.

WILSON

Off to work?

LUNA

Yep.

> Wilson nods and returns to his writing. Then on a sudden impulse he looks up.

WILSON

Luna? I'm awfully busy and we hardly ever talk these days. I hope you know I love you as much as ever.

LUNA

Of course I know that.

WILSON

It's Crowleymas tonight, so don't be surprised to find the house full of witches and wizards when you get home.

LUNA

When am I ever surprised?

> She kisses him on the forehead.

Bye, Dad.

> Arlen and Bob prepare for a party. Crowley wanders through with his accordion.

CROWLEY
(singing)

A feast for the first night of the Prophet and his Bride!
A feast for the three days of the writing of the *Book of the Law.*
A feast for fire and a feast for water; a feast for life and a greater feast for death!
Do what thou wilt shall be the whole of the law. Love is the law, love under will.

WILSON
(narration)

Crowleymas 1974 – October 12, a date associated with an Italian navigator who introduced slavery to the New World and syphilis to the Old – was celebrated at our apartment house with weird and eldritch festivities. Arlen and I, representing the Discordian Society, together with Stephen upstairs (reformed Druids of North America), Claire and Carol in another apartment (witches, New Reformed Order of the Golden Dawn) and the Great Wild Beast Furtherment Society (which is really Stephen and me and another neighbour named Charles) opened all our rooms to a Crowleymas party and invited nearly 100 local wizards, mystics and scientists.

                    (to audience)

And here you all are.

> The music strikes up. Arlen and Wilson chat to the audience and hand round drinks as guests begin to mingle.

WILSON

Jacques! It's fantastic that you've made it. A very good Crowleymas to you. This is Paul. Paul, Jacques Vallee – he's the leading expert on the UFO mystery.

PAUL

And what is the solution to the mystery then, Jacques?

ARLEN

Alright, Paul. Let me get the man a drink before the inquisition begins. What are you having Jacques?

JACQUES

I am hoping you will have some of that marvellous mushroom brew as you did last year?

ARLEN

Yes of course.

WILSON

I wanted to talk to you about an extraordinary meeting I had with Timothy Leary last week.

JACQUES

Oh yes?

WILSON

Yes, he's got quite a thing going on at Vacaville, a group of fellow inmates have been conducting experiments in telepathy with extraterrestrials with some hair-raising results. They have generated a whole stack of material that Leary is calling The Starseed Transmissions. The similarity between that and Crowley's *Book of the Law* revelations are startling.

JACQUES

I'd love to take a look at that material.

WILSON

Grady! Phyllis!

    (to a group of audience)

This is Grady and his wife, Phyllis. Grady is Caliph of the Ordo Templi Orientis.

PAUL

So, what are your findings from your UFO research then?

ARLEN

Here you are, Jacques. Finest mushroom tea.

    (to audience member)

Would you like this cup?

    Others arrive.

Oh hi, Grady and Phyllis. This is Tom, Jacques, my wife Arlen. And this is Michael and Paul – they are leading experts in longevity research, particularly cryogenic preservation. What can I get you all?

> The party noise gets loud and boisterous for a moment. We can only make out the following speech.

GRADY

That's the $64,000 question. For years I've been asking Phyllis and everybody else I know: Why does the Gnosis always get busted? Every single time the energy is raised and large-scale group illuminations are occurring, the local branch of the Inquisition kills it dead. Why? I'll tell you what I think. The Higher Intelligences, whoever they are, aren't all playing on the same team. Some of them are trying to encourage our evolution to higher levels and some of them want to keep us stuck just where we are. You see, some occult lodges – not naming any names – are working with the evolution accelerators, and some are working with the other intelligences.

ARLEN

But, Grady, correct me if I'm wrong, this is a pretty standard paranoia amongst all adepts, that some of the other paths belong to the Black Brotherhood of the evil path.

GRADY

All I know is paranoid magicians outlive the others.

> They laugh.
>
> Kerry Thornley bursts in.

KERRY

Listen you assholes. I'm the most important man on the planet – I am the only one who knows all about the Kennedy assassination.

> This kills the conversation and music dead.

WILSON

OK, Kerry. Come on in.

KERRY

OK, I admit I thought it was all coincidence. But now I'm sure I was manipulated while I was in the Marines. I was set up just like my old pal Oswald – I was set up as a fall guy to drive investigators like Garrison off the real scent. Like old Brother in Law said, the best technique to kill the president was to use individuals who didn't even know they were being used. That conversation we had about how to kill JFK, I reckon it was a test; a test to see if I had any memory of the brainwashing that had already taken place.

>   Wilson holds Kerry's
>   shoulders and tries to
>   establish eye contact

>   WILSON

Kerry, it's good to see you.

>   KERRY
>   (whispering)

Your whole Starseed thing with Leary? That's been infiltrated.

>   WILSON
>   (taken aback)

How the hell do you know about that?

>   KERRY

Because I overheard one of the agents that's been tailing me.

>   WILSON

Jesus, Kerry.

>   KERRY

The last party I was at I got pistol whipped by masked bandits who stole all my ID. They only took money from everyone else.

>   ARLEN

Sit down, Kerry. Let me get you a drink or something.

>   KERRY
>   (lunging for Arlen)

Don't treat me like a fucking mental patient.

> The crowd reacts with hostility to this attack on Arlen.

And warn everyone that there may be a second Thornley wandering around. Anyone who shows up with my ID is an impersonator. And another thing, Bob. Why did you dedicate that fucking *Illuminatus* book to me? Now any attempts I make to reveal the truth are just put down to publicity gimmicks for the book. It's Operation Mindfuck, don't you get it?

WILSON

What does Greg say about all this, Kerry?

KERRY

He said, "If they prove that you are CIA, demand back pay".

WILSON

I think your imagination is growing faster than your evidence, Kerry.

KERRY

Listen, I know all about you, Bob. You're part of the assassination conspiracy team. You're my CIA baby-sitter.

WILSON

Kerry, I'm just Bob.

KERRY

Are you trying to tell me that you haven't been to Atlanta to give me LSD to remove the programming the Navy had administered when I was in the Marines?

WILSON

That's exactly what I'm telling you.

KERRY

Oh Christ – they've brainwashed you as well.

ARLEN

Bob, should we call someone?

KERR
(lunging again)

No don't you call anyone, you hear me Arlen?

(leaving)

Look into the case of Robert Byron Watson, that's all I'm saying. You watch your back, Bob. If I find out you're working for the CIA, you just better watch yourself.

ARLEN
(very angry)

Get out, Kerry.

KERRY exits.

JACQUES

Jesus, poor guy. You think it's clinical paranoia?

WILSON

Oh, he's clinically paranoid. But in my estimation Kerry Thornley still knows 99% more about the real nature of the American Government than most of us ever will. We both invoked Eris as our Goddess supreme, and we both got drawn into Operation Mindfuck. You either emerge agnostic or paranoid.

ARLEN

I'm really starting to worry about his fixation with you, Bob. All those letters denouncing you and now he just shows up.

WILSON

It's not ideal.

GRADY

All conspiracy buffs are persecuted eventually. It's a sociological law I'd stake my life on.

JACQUES

Or maybe you had it right in *Illuminatus* and every conspiracy ever imagined actually exists.

WILSON

Well, the fact remains that those who believe the world is run by Jesuits get persecuted as much as those who believe it's run by the Elders of Zion; and those who believe it is run by the Rockefellers also get persecuted in equal measure. There almost seems to be a neurotic-psionic law: whatever you fear most will eventually come after you.

> Suddenly a policeman is standing amidst the revellers.

POLICEMAN

Are you Mr Wilson?

> Wilson looks nervous, aware of all the drugs that are being taken behind him.

WILSON

Yes?

POLICEMAN

Is your wife there too?

WILSON

Yes, Officer can I ask what this is regarding?

POLICEMAN

Are you in the middle of a party?

WILSON

Yes, has there been some kind of a complaint?

POLICEMAN

No Sir, I just think you and your wife might like to be somewhere quiet where you can sit down.

>They leave the throng of the party and go to a quiet spot.

ARLEN
(joining them)

Is something wrong?

WILSON

I think something is terribly wrong.

POLICEMAN

Is there somewhere we can sit down?

>The party is in full swing behind them.

WILSON

Is it Graham?

POLICEMAN

Shall we go out here?

> They move away from the party.

It's about your daughter. Luna. I'm sorry. Your daughter is dead.

WILSON
(quietly)

Oh, God, no.

> Shocked silence.

> A tripped out party-goer comes over.

TRIPPER

Is everything OK?

POLICEMAN

Please go back inside. I think you may want to pass the word that it's time for everyone to go home.

TRIPPER

Is it a bust?

WILSON
(shouting)

Just tell them that the goddamn party is over!

> The tripper goes back inside, traumatised. Everyone leaves except Michael and Paul.

ARLEN

Where is my baby now?

POLICEMAN

She's at the city morgue.

ARLEN

I need to be with her.

POLICEMAN

We can go down there now. I need to warn you – she's been badly beaten up.

                           WILSON

She's been beaten?

                         POLICEMAN

Yes, your daughter was murdered.

                              The sound of Arlen's anguish,
                              as the scene dissolves.

3.4: THE MORGUE

> Suddenly they are standing in the morgue, Luna's lifeless body under a white sheet.

WILSON

We were very, very lucky to have that Clear Light shining within our family for 15 years. We must never stop being grateful for that, even in our grief.

> The policeman enters quietly.

POLICEMAN

I'm sorry to disturb you, but I thought you'd want to know that the main suspect has been caught.

WILSON

Thank you.

> The body of Luna is wheeled off, the lights shift and they are suddenly back in their kitchen.

3.5: THE PARTY'S OVER

>Sitting somberly in the living room are cybernetisists Michael and Paul.

ARLEN

Are they still here?

>Michael and Paul look up embarrassed, and full of sadness.

ARLEN

I'm going upstairs. I've got to phone Karuna. And I suppose I should phone Graham's camp leader.

>She exits.

WILSON

She was murdered. By a Sioux Indian. I've seen him around Berkeley a few times. An alcoholic. Apparently well known to the police. Always making threats and grandiose claims that he would do something great for his people. I suppose in his mind he was getting even for Wounded Knee when he beat my daughter to death.

MICHAEL

We're so sorry.

WILSON

The guys who dropped napalm on the Vietnamese children thought they were protecting their homes from the barbarian hordes of gooks. Gurdjieff used to say, "Fairness? Decency? How can you expect fairness and decency on a planet of sleeping people?"

PAUL

Luna was just the most wonderful person.

WILSON

This is going to be worse, much worse than any other bereavement I have known. This is of a different order of hellishness. Losing my dad, or my brother or my friends just doesn't compare to losing a child I have adored since birth.

MICHAEL
(gently)

Bob, we know you're in complete shock. But have you considered cryonic preservation for Luna's body?

WILSON
(coming out of his reverie)

We don't have that kind of money.

PAUL

Bob, we've made a few phone calls – I hope you don't mind. Everyone at the Bay Area Cryonics Society would be happy to donate their labour for free.

MICHAEL

We already have enough pledges to cover the first year's expenses . . .

WILSON

Pledges? Who?

PAUL

People who appreciate your writings on longevity and immortality and want to help you now.

WILSON

My God.

MICHAEL

We'd need to act fast.

WILSON

I need to speak to Arlen.

> Paul and Michael exit.
> Arlen enters.

ARLEN

Karuna is on her way.

WILSON

Is Karuna OK to travel?

ARLEN

She's on her way.

WILSON
(stumbling and awkward)

Arlen. Paul and Michael have suggested that we could . . . cryogenically preserve Luna's body.

ARLEN

Jesus Christ Bob! It's all your insane ideas and experiments that have led us here. Our daughter is dead and all you can do is try and escape to some kind of futuristic fantasy. Our daughter is dead, Bob! Don't you realise?

> She storms out. A long pause. Wilson is frozen in grief.
>
> Arlen appears again in the door.

ARLEN

I'm so sorry. I'm so sorry. If Luna taught us one thing, it was to stop the Wheel of Karma. To take bad energy and turn it into good energy before passing it on. Say yes. Even if it doesn't work for Luna it all contributes to scientific knowledge.

WILSON

Oh my darling.

> They hug for a long time.

I'll let Paul and Michael know.

> He goes back downstairs. Picks up the phone and dials.

(down phone)

We'd like to go ahead.

PAULA
(elsewhere, on phone)

OK. We'll need to consult a lawyer before we confront the coroner and the DA. One false move and we'll lose the gamble.

MICHAEL

We'll let you know how we get on.

WILSON

Thank you.

> The sound of Luna's young voice.

LUNA (V.O.)

Daddy, can I have some foot doot?

WILSON

"Most sacrilegious murder hath broke ope the Lord's anointed temple."

I find myself remembering over and over, the famous lines from Macbeth: "Most sacrilegious murder hath broke ope The Lord's anointed temple."

The most elegant formulation of Bell's Theorem is that there is no true separation anywhere.

Send not to ask for whom the bell tolls; it tolls for thee.

When the King of Wu sent Confucious into exile, many disciples followed the philosopher, but in later years one of them said he wished he could see his home again.

"How is it far," Confucious asked, "if you can think of it?" How is it far, if you can think of it?

> The phone rings suddenly and abruptly. Lights up on Michael on the other end of the line.

MICHAEL
(down phone)

We've just left the coroner's office. He obviously needs to meet with you and Arlen, but he turned out to be a broad-minded man. He seemed quite captured by the idea of the cryonic gamble.

WILSON

Should we come down there now?

MICHAEL

The sooner the better.

WILSON

OK. We're on our way.

Arlen enters.

ARLEN

Was that Graham?

WILSON

No, darling. That was Michael. They've got the go-ahead from the coroner, but he needs to meet with us.

ARLEN

I'll get my coat.

WILSON

Arlen. It'll almost certainly not come to anything. And not within our lifetimes.

ARLEN

You told me yourself, Bob. However you calculate the odds on cryonic preservation, and whatever way you estimate scientific advance, you come out with a chance above zero.

WILSON

Burial or cremation gives you a chance of exactly zero.

ARLEN

A 0.001 percent chance is still a chance, Bob. Where is my coat?

WILSON

It's on the hook.

ARLEN

I need to write a note for Karuna. Give me a minute. I wish Graham would call.

The phone rings again.

WILSON

Hello?

ARLEN

Is it Graham?

Wilson shakes his head, no.

MICHAEL
(down phone)

Bob, I'm so sorry – we –it's Luna's body– she's– we just feel –well, I've had some experts take a look, and well – it's very decomposed. I'm so sorry, Bob. Cryonic preservation of her body is virtually pointless.

WILSON

I see.

ARLEN

What's wrong?

WILSON

Her body's decomposed too far –

MICHAEL

I suggest preservation of the brain.

WILSON

He suggests we preserve her brain.

ARLEN

Do it.

                        Lights fade.

3.6: FUNERAL

> Spotlight on Bob speaking from a podium.

WILSON
(finishing a story)

– and then she said, "magick is just trying on different costumes to see what the effects are."

> Pause

So, Luna Wilson, who tried to paint the Clear Light and was the kindest child I have ever known is dead.

How many fathers and mothers, in this cruelly insane century, have wept over murdered children as Arlen and I have wept? And continue to weep.

But as much as I want it to, my rage won't settle only on the murderer. I cannot think of him without seeing him as the resultant of all the horrors and atrocities committed against the Native Americans since we whites first arrived here. My rage goes right through him and past him to include the whole structure of Christian bigotry, white racism and capitalist greed that had made the genocide of the Native Americans inevitable – and the high alcoholism and violence rate of the survivors equally inevitable.

Luna is the first ever murder victim to go on a cryonic time-trip to possible resuscitation.

We are the first family in history to attempt to cancel the God-like power which every murderer takes into his hands when he decides to terminate life.

Above all, by this scientific endeavour we express and commemorate our faith in life and our total rejection of death and violence. By this attempt to preserve life, we say "No" to the dealers in death and violence. We say "No" to the governments that use mass murder as policy. We say "No" to an entertainment industry based on the pornography of violence and the prurience of sadism. And we say "No" to the creature who, in his blind ignorance of the value of life, killed Luna to steal a few dollars.

3.7: LIVERPOOL PERFORMANCE

MISS PORTINARI

The Last Judgement: Trump 20. But as I've explained, because the order of the tarot was reversed, the true secret is that it's actually second. This is the nightmare to which the soul awakes if it begins, even in the slightest, to question reality as defined by society. This is an internal discovery – this whole trip is an internal voyage – and this is merely the second stage. But if one thinks of the story as the story of the external world, and if the order is as it normally is, then this comes as the penultimate Armageddon with Trump 21 to follow: the Kingdom of the Saints.

Meanwhile, backstage

KEN

Listen. I just had a piss with Peter Hall and he's raving about it all. He's saying they're going to have *Illuminatus* open the new space at the National Theatre!

Excited cheers of approval

It's because you're all heroes. You felt the beckoning of your destinies and you followed the clues all the way to a squat in a caff in Liverpool. You plumbed the toilets, learned these crazy lines, made your costumes and your sets. You know what you're doing here is mythic don't you? You've risen above the 99% of bollocks into the 1% of divine and glorious bollocks! I mean, if we don't keep the great tradition of Impossibly Complex, Over-Long, Slung-On theatre alive – then who the fuck will?

Listen, I'm going to phone Wilson and Shea. We've got to get them over for the opening at the National Theatre. The National Theatre, chaps!

>On stage.

MISS PORTINARI

This is the error of the apocalyptic sects, and of the Illuminati from Weishaupt to Hitler, which lead to an attempt to actually carry it out, with ovens for the Jews and gypsies and other "inferiors" and the promise of a Brave New World for the pure, faithful, and Aryan afterward. Do you see what I mean about confusing the map with the territory? The next card is the Sun, which really means Osiris Risen – or in terms of the offshoot of the Osirian religion most popular in the last two milleniums, Jesus Risen. This is what happens if you survive the last Judgement, or Dark Night of the Soul, without becoming some kind of fanatic or lunatic. Eventually, if you miss those attractive and pernicious alternatives, the redemptive force appears: the eternal Sun. Once again, if you project this outward and think that the Sun in the sky, or some Sun-like divine man has redeemed you, you can lapse into lunacy or fanatism. In Hitler's case it was Karl Haushofer.

For most of the nuts on the street, it's Jesus. So it goes. Those who do not confuse the levels realise it's the redemptive force within themselves and pass on to Key 18, the Moon . . .

> Meanwhile, backstage. Ken is on the phone. Actors are gathered around to hear what happens.

KEN

It's ringing and ringing. Oh hello? Is that Arlen? It's Ken Campbell here. Great news. *Illuminatus* is going to the Royal National Theatre! I want to get Bob over for the opening.

> Long pause as Ken listens.

Oh Christ. I'm so sorry. I – I'll let you go, Arlen. We're all thinking of you both.

HAGBARD ACTOR

Is he coming over?

KEN

His daughter was murdered.

> The cast react with shock.

Apparently he's hardly moved since the funeral. He hasn't written anything. Arlen thought it would be good for him to come, but they haven't got any money at all.

PRUE

Oh God, it's so awful.

KEN
(with sudden resolve)

He has to come over. He has to see what he's created.

HAGBARD ACTOR

Shouldn't the National pay to fly him and Shea over? Or the British Council?

KEN

They should, but they bloody well won't. Let's have a whip-round! I'll tell Bob Shea what we're doing and he can sort himself out and we'll all tell Bob that the British Council paid for it. Our own little conspiracy.

On stage.

MISS PORTINARI

Last is the Fool, Key 0. He walks over the edge of the cliff, careless of the danger. In short, he has conquered death. Nothing can frighten him, and he can never be enslaved. It's the end of the trip, and keeping humanity from getting there is the chief business of every governing group.

JOE

And that's it. Twenty-two stages. Not twenty-three. Thank God we got away from that number for a while.

MISS PORTINARI

No. Tarot is an anagram of rota, remember? The extra T reminds you that the wheel turns back to rejoin itself. There is a twenty-third step, and it's right where you started, only now you face it without fear.

3.8: GRIEF AND POVERTY

> Wilson is staring in the mirror.

ARLEN

Bob?

WILSON

Why in God's name did I ever quit *Playboy*? We were happy then. Why didn't you stop me making a Goddamn mess of everything?

ARLEN

Don't do this, Bob.

WILSON

You said it, Arlen – it was all my damned stupid experiments that got us evicted and led to this squalid, hopeless, God-forsaken slum –

ARLEN

Bob, stop it. I never meant that.

WILSON

We'll never afford Graham's college fees. Karuna needs help and we can't give it to her. The boiler's fucked up, your medical insurance needs renewing. I've lost count how much I owe the IRS. We're in our 50s, Arlen, we're still on welfare and they're trying to take that from us.

ARLEN

I know that, Bob. Perhaps you could rest for a bit? It might all not seem so bad after some sleep.

WILSON

According to William Buckley, this poverty is supposed to build character and keep America strong. I bet he was never poor a single day in his life. We'd all be less paranoid and hopeless if instead of being poor seven days a week, we could be comfortable for six days and subjected to Chinese Water Torture on the seventh.

ARLEN
(laughs weakly)

I guess you're right.

Pause.

WILSON

I can hear her talking to me at night, Arlen.

ARLEN

Me too.

WILSON

I want her back. If I'd just stayed at *Playboy* she wouldn't have needed to work at that shop for some extra money, because her dad could have provided her with everything. If I'd not been so ego-driven to become a failure of an author, a failure of a father, a failure of a husband. Had my head turned by all this mumbo jumbo. The whole cryonic thing is just a bunch of screwball technocrats. Luna is dead and this cryonic attempt to evade that is as sad an example of wishful thinking as all the doctrines of heaven and hell and reincarnation. I'm deluded again, tricked again, as always.

Wilson breaks down completely.

ARLEN

It's alright. It's alright.

WILSON
(sobbing)

The whole world has turned into a lesson in the futility of hope.

ARLEN
(suddenly stern)

Bob, this is what all your work has been for. All the rituals, the loving heart exercises, the re-imprinting, the meta-programming. It was all for this moment. You have a choice to make right here. Love or fear.

WILSON

I'm so scared, Arlen. I can't see how we'll ever get through this.

> Pause.

> In the distance the phone rings. When it's obvious it won't stop, Arlen exits to answer it.

WILSON

Total, abject, complete failure.

> Tears are rolling down his cheeks.

> After a few moments Arlen returns.

ARLEN

That was Ken Campbell on the phone. The British Council want to fly you and Bob Shea to London for the premiere of *Illuminatus*. I think it's a sign, Bob.

WILSON

There's absolutely no way I'm going.

3.9: THE NATIONAL THEATRE

Wilson and Shea arrive backstage at the National Theatre clutching their luggage.

The goat boy greets them, naked and covered in blood.

ACTOR

Mr Wilson? Mr Shea? This is the greatest honour. Your book has completely changed my life.

SHEA

So I see.

ACTOR

I'll find Ken.

Actor exits

SHEA

We're here, Bob.

WILSON

It's like the greatest Discordian joke ever. This whole totally subversive ritual staged under the patronage of

Her Royal Majesty the Queen of England – it's nectar and ambrosia, Bob.

PRUE

Hi, I'm Prue. You must be Robert and Bob? I'm playing Eris. I'm so happy to meet you both. Can you believe we made it here?

WILSON

We were just saying.

KEN

Mr Wilson! Mr Shea! Gentlemen, welcome to the greatest show on Planet World. The next 11 and a half hours are going to make you both very proud.

> A crew member enters

This is George Harvey Webb – he oversaw the satanic rituals for us – made sure they were fully authentic. He once met Aleister Crowley on a train.

WEBB

An honour, gentlemen.

KEN

That's Mitch – he's in charge of dolphins and golden apples.

> Mitch walks past briskly with a giant golden apple.

MITCH

They keep deflating, Ken.

> Chris enters.

KEN

Chris, co-writer and playing George Dorn.

CHRIS

How wonderful to finally meet you both. We have lived and breathed your book and it's blown our minds.

KEN

Yeah, that was the main reason for slinging it on, really. To have an excuse to live in your book.

SHEA

(with a wink)

We're delighted that the British Council saw fit to fly us over. I'm going to find the little boys room – If I'm going to be glued to my seat for 11 and a half hours I need to prepare.

VOICEOVER

Ladies and gentlemen of the *Illuminatus* company. This is your 23 minute call. 23 minutes please, thank you.

KEN

Yeah, we made them change it to that.

WILSON

Well, I'd better let you get on with it.

PRUE

No, Bob, stay. Have a smoke.

WILSON

I can't refuse Eris herself.

KEN
(to someone offstage as he exits)

Well tell the cunt that they have to lower the apple down from the rigging, or how's it going to be there in time for Chris to fuck it?

> Wilson drinks it in. They light up the joint.

PRUE

We were all so sorry to hear about Luna.

WILSON

Thanks for saying that.

PRUE

It's wonderful that you've come over. The whole company are completely thrilled. You're our hero.

STAGEHAND

There's a telegram for Mr Wilson. From a Dr Leary?

WILSON

Thank you.

WEBB

Is that from Timothy Leary?

WILSON

That's right."YOU ARE SURROUNDED BY A NETWORK OF LOVE AND GRATITUDE. WE ARE ALL WITH YOU AND SUPPORT YOU. PS. I'M A FREE MAN BABY."

>   Cheers go up from those
>   gathered. The lights go down.

>   VOICEOVER

7 hours later.

>   The lights go up.

>   VOICEOVER

Act 23 Beginners, please. Ms Gee, Mr Cunningham, Mr Langham – this is your call. Act 23 Beginners please, thank you.

3.10: ON STAGE

Onboard Hagbard's golden submarine.

GEORGE

I've got to warn you, I come from a long line of labor agitators and Reds. You'll never convert me to a right-wing position. You're just a gang of objectivists.

MAVIS

Objectivists? We're anarchists and outlaws, goddamn it. Didn't you understand that much?

HAGBARD

We've got nothing to do with right-wing, left-wing or any other half-assed political category. If you work within the system, you come to one of the either/or choices that were implicit in the system from the beginning. You're talking like a medieval serf, asking the first agnostic whether he worships God or the Devil.

MAVIS

We're outside the system's categories. You'll never get the hang of our game if you keep thinking in flat-earth imagery of right and left, good and evil, up and down.

                    HAGBARD

If you need a group label for us, we're political
non-Euclideans. But even that's not true. Sink me, nobody
on this submarine agrees with anybody else about anything,
except maybe what the fellow with the horns told the old
man in the clouds:
                    MAVIS & HAGBARD
Non serviam!

                                        Backstage.

                                        Wilson pops in to
                                        compliment the cast.

                    WILSON

Great job guys!

                                        Suddenly there's a load of
                                        bustle as the actors begin to
                                        prepare for the Black Mass
                                        Scene.

                    PRUE

Bob? We're hoping you'll come and take part in the Black
Mass scene?

                    WILSON

No, I –

                    PRUE

This is Eris speaking, Bob.

                    WILSON
                (managing a smile)

Well, OK. What's the costume?

247

                              ACTOR

Naked and covered in goat's blood.

                              WILSON

I don't know.

                              PRUE

Ok, you can wear this.

                              She hands him a black robe.

We dare you Bob.

3.11: BLACK MASS SCENE

The whole cast enter in black robes, droning. Wilson is amongst them, looking a little stagestruck.

George Harvey-Webb steps forward now dressed as Satanic priest, Pederastia. Or is he Crowley or the actor who plays him playing someone else? Who can tell anymore?

>PEDERASTIA

God is dead.

>CROWLEY

God is dead.

>PEDERASTIA
>(more dramatically)

God is dead. We are all absolutely free.

>CROWLEY

God is dead. We are all absolutely free.

PEDERASTIA

Do what thou wilt shall be the whole of the law.

CROWLEY

Do what thou wilt shall be the whole of the law.

PEDERASTIA

Welcome all to the Lake Shore Drive Chapter. I find this part of the ceremony most distasteful. If only our father below would allow a boy on the altar, instead of that girl, when I'm officiating. But alas, he's very rigid about such things. As usual, therefore, I'll ask the newest recruit to take my place for this part of the ceremony.

> Everyone steps aside leaving George Dorn front and centre.

It's quite simple. You just take this communion wafer, it's a fully consecrated host, I stole it from the church myself.

You take this and you . . . (whispers)

GEORGE DORN
(startled)

What?

CROWLEY

Yes, that's right. And then you . . .

(whispers)

> George moves uncertainly towards the altar. He pauses for a moment then continues toward the altar.

The sacrificial woman appears on the altar.

CROWLEY

Eee-oh. Eh!

George bends over and performs cunnilingus on the woman. She arches her back rhythmically in an athletic style, and her legs slowly extend and extend, reaching across the audience's heads. The legs begin to shake.

CAST

Eeeoh. Eh!

> They move around the altar, chanting in time with the woman's pelvic gyrations.

PEDERASTIA

Oh sunafarasaji

CROWLEY

Oh sunafarasaji

PEDERASTIA

Yogge Sthothene blodzin

CROWLEY

Yogge Sthotheneblodzin.

PEDERASTIA AND CROWLEY

By Ashtoreth. By Pan Pangenitor. By the Yellow Sign. By the gifts I have made; and the powers I have purchased. By him who is not to be named.

> PEDERASTIA makes the sign of the beast.

PEDERASTIA

By Sammaiel. By Amonand Ra. Vente, vente Lucifer.

> Satan appears all around them. They cower and cover their eyes. The woman continues to moan. The E-O-E continues throughout Satan's speech.

SATAN/FUCKUP

OK, OK. We don't have to get touchy and hostile with each other over a few little theatrics. Just tell me what sort of business transaction you went and dragged me up here for, and I'm sure we can work out all the details in a down home, business-like, cards-on-the-table fashion, with no hard feelings and mutual satisfaction all round.

> One of the coven becomes hysterical and screams.

ACTOR

Quiet, you fool You don't want to give it more power.

PEDERASTIA
(to screaming initiate)

Your tongue is sealed till I release it

> The initiate strains noiselessly to scream.

COVEN

Do what thou wilt! Do what thou wilt! AGIOS O BAPHOMET! Satanas – venire! Hear me, you Dark Gods! Prince of Darkness, hear my oath! I am yours!

> The coven do what thou wilt to each other.
>
> Absolute Frenzy.
>
> Then the mayhem becomes slow motion, and Wilson stands in the centre of the swirling mass of Satanists.

> One of the cast steps out of the mayhem, and stands opposite Wilson. They remove their hood. It is Arlen.

ARLEN

It was all for this moment. You have a choice to make right here. Love or fear.

WILSON

I choose an open heart. I choose to love all beings. I love the officials who rejected our welfare claim. I love the grinding poverty. I love the system which keeps us poor while others accumulate enormous wealth. I love Kerry who hounds us daily with his insanity. I love the guy who sent us a bomb threat because he thought I was head of the Illuminati. I love Buckley and Rockefeller and Nixon. I love the man who murdered my daughter.

> Tears are rolling down his cheeks.

A network of love . . . right here on stage in the midst of a Satanic ritual at Her Majesty's Royal National Theatre! Crowley, you Great Beast – how much of this was programmed before I was even born? It's a new imprint – a network of love!

> Three hooded figures approach Wilson and lead him to The White Room: a vision of the Magi throughout the ages looking back at us beyond the veil of the stage.
>
> Lights up on Luna.

LUNA

Let it be known that there exists, unsuspected by the great crowd, a very ancient Order whose object is the spiritual evolution of mankind by means of conquering falsehood and fear. Into the Sacred Society no man or woman may be admitted unless they enter it themselves by virtue of their inner illumination. In the spiritual realm, the only conquest left is that of the self.

3.12: FINAL WORD

The Gates of Chapel Perilous.

Wilson is unceremoniously shoved through the gates on to the stage. He is older Bob.

OLD WILSON

Oh it's you lot. I vaguely remember you from a dream I had about being in a cryptic and ambiguous play.

Pause.

My darling Arlen died five years ago.

I have lost several friends in the last couple of years (Leary and Burroughs are gone). But I'm still so optimistic that it seriously annoys ecologists – and Marxists – and other people who think we are only "moral" if we are deeply worried and habitually angry.

There is a common misperception about Cosmic Trigger: many people think that I believe some of the metaphors and models employed here. Listen, I set out on a course of induced brain change, and like most others who've attempted this path, I soon found myself in metaphysical hot water. It became urgently obvious that my previous models and metaphors would not account for what I was experiencing and I had run out of map. I therefore had to create new models and metaphors as I went along, but, and I want to make this more clear than ever: I do not believe anything. Anything. It seems to be a hangover of the medieval Catholic era that causes most people, even the educated, to think that everybody must believe something; that if one is not a theist, one must be a dogmatic atheist, and if one does not think that capitalism is perfect, one must believe fervently in socialism. My own opinion – and it is only an opinion – is that belief is the death of intelligence – or as Kerry put it: Convictions cause convicts.

This notion that "my current model of the world contains the whole universe and will never need to be revised" appears so primitive, so arrogant and absurd to me that I am perpetually astonished that people still manage to live with such a medieval attitude.

Our lonely little selves can be illuminated or flooded with radical science-fiction style information and cosmic perspectives, and the source of this may be those extraterrestrials who seemed to be helping me at times, or it may be the Secret Chiefs of Sufism, or the parapsychologists/computers of the 23rd Century beaming data backward in time, or it may just be the unactivated parts of our own brains. Despite the current reign of our New Inquisition, which attempts to halt research in this area, we will learn more about that as time passes. Meanwhile agnosticism is both honest and becomingly modest.

Oh, this made me laugh. Recently the Natural Surrealist Party began running a chap named George Papoon for

President. Papoon went around with a paper bag over his head and used the campaign slogan "not insane!". Somehow I got on their mailing list and began to receive a series of press releases about the Doggiez from Sirius, who are allegedly at large in our midst. I don't know if there's any here tonight?

Some audience members will bark and howl.

This is all a joke, of course, just as Illuminatus was when Shea and I first conceived it.

And probably the Papoon people will think I am a bit

259

over-imaginative if I suggest that none of us can even begin to understand what a joke really is.. or where they really come from.

> A letter is chucked on stage. Wilson slowly manoeuvres himself to pick it up.

In 1975 I lost the ability to know when something was about to come through the door. It wasn't all that useful a skill anyway.

> He opens the envelope.

It's a cheque for $23. How funny.

> Another letter plops through the letterbox.

It's another cheque for $23.

> And another.

And another. OK, there's something fishy going on. Time to consult the oracle.

> He fires up his laptop.

Type in Robert Anton Wilson 23 dollars. And . . .magick.

> (reading)

"Ok guys, time to support cosmic thinking patriarch Robert Anton Wilson, whose infirmity and depleted finances have put him in the precarious position of not being able to meet next month's rent or his medical costs. His last wish is to die in his home, but he cannot afford this option. Robert Anton Wilson will one day be remembered alongside such literary philosophers as Aldous Huxley and James Joyce."

I don't know about that.

"But right now, Bob is a human being in a rather painful flesh-suit, who needs our help. I refuse for the history books to say he died alone and destitute, for I want future generations to know we appreciated Robert Anton Wilson while he was alive. If Bob Wilson changed your life, send him $23 dollars now."

> A letter is tossed onstage, followed immediately by another, and another. The cast appear amongst the audience, scattering letters like confetti.

RISING CACOPHONY OF VOICES
(PRE-RECORDED V.O.)

Your work completely changed my life, Bob. If it wasn't for you I don't know what course my life would have taken etc etc . . .

> NB: These were snippets of audio recordings of actual fans expressing their love for Bob.

WILSON

When Leary got word – after having been a free man for only a short while – that his appeal had been rejected and he may have to go back to jail, I remember somebody asked him, "What do you do, Dr Leary, when somebody keeps giving you negative energy?"

LEARY

Come back at them with all the positive energy you have.

WILSON

And so I learned the final secret of the Illuminati.

                              MUSIC: Inquire Within

EVERYONE

Inquire within! Inquire Within.
You never know what you might find.
Unscrew the inscrutable. Think the Unthinkable.
Dive down to the roots of your mind.
Inquire Within, Inquire Within.
Just don't believe all that you've seen.
Use your perception to answer the question:
Who is the master who makes the grass green?

Inquire Within.

END

Cast 2017

Robert Anton Wilson – Oliver Senton

Arlen Wilson – Kate Alderton

The Goddess Eris – Claudia Boulton

Timothy Leary – Jethro Skinner

Robert Shea – Tom Baker

Ken Campbell – Josh Darcy

Kerry Thornley – Lee Ravitz

Luna Wilson – Dixie McDevitt

Prunella Gee – Carrie Marx

Greg Hill – Leigh Kelly

Other characters were played by members of the cast.

Additional 2014 Cast Members:

Katy-Anne Bellis, Andrew Macbean, Robert Waters, Tim Newton, Nick Marcq, Pete Wilson

Crew 2017

Director – Daisy Campbell

Producers – Michelle Watson, Dave Wybrow, Dominic Search, Kate Alderton, Michelle Olley, Claudia Boulton

Stage Manager – Nadia Luijten

Design – Amoeba, John Horabin

Lighting – Chris Lincé

Music Director – Robert Burnham

Musical contributors – Fayann Smith, Tom Baker, Space Blaster, Steve Fly, Megan Clifton

Particular thanks to Jon Harris, Jonathan Greet, Alan Moore, Myra Stuart, Deb Jones, Bethany Pratt, Thea-Ellida Eike, Larry Sidorczuk, Matt Baker-Jones, Alistair Fruish, Irving Rappaport, Simon Annand, Nic Alderton, Phil Clucas

Endless thanks to so, so many more. You know who you are, you Cosmic Cats. Without you, gnothing.

It takes a village to pull a Cosmic Trigger.

You should view the world as a conspiracy run by a very closely-knit group of nearly omnipotent people, and you should think of those people as yourself and your friends.

– Robert Anton Wilson

More information about the 2014 and 2017 productions – including many more photographs – can be found at www.cosmictriggerplay.com

Tune In. Turn On. Find The Others.

Publishing the Books of Robert Anton Wilson
and Other Adventurous Thinkers

www.hilaritaspress.com

www.ingramcontent.com/pod-product-compliance
Lightning Source LLC
Chambersburg PA
CBHW041125110526
44592CB00020B/2690